Our Family Meeting Book

Fun and Easy Ways to Manage Time, Build Communication, and Share Responsibility Week by Week

Elaine Hightower & Betsy Riley

Foreword by Michele Borba, Ed.D.

free spirit PUBLISHING® Works for kids®

D1500490

Library of Congress Cataloging-in-Publication Data

Hightower, Elaine, 1959-
   Our family meeting book : fun and easy ways to manage time, build communication, and share responsibility week by week / by Elaine Hightower and Betsy Riley.
      p. cm.
Includes bibliographical references and index.
ISBN 1-57542-120-8
1. Family. 2. Family—Time management. 3. Communication in the family. I. Riley, Betsy. II. Title.

HQ518 .H544 2002
306.85—dc21

2002010075

At the time of this book's publication, all facts and figures cited are the most current available; all telephone numbers, addresses, and Web site URLs are accurate and active; all publications, organizations, Web sites, and other resources exist as described in this book; and all have been verified as of January 2004. The authors and Free Spirit Publishing make no warranty or guarantee concerning the information and materials given out by organizations or content found at Web sites, and we are not responsible for any changes that occur after this book's publication. If you find an error or believe that a resource listed here is not as described, please contact Free Spirit Publishing. Parents, teachers, and other adults: We strongly urge you to monitor children's use of the Internet.

The excerpts on pages 12 and 34 are from *Building Moral Intelligence: The Seven Essential Virtues that Teach Kids to Do the Right Thing* by Michele Borba, Ed.D., copyright © 2001 by Michele Borba. Reprinted by permission of John Wiley & Sons, Inc.

The quotes on pages 22 and 68 are from *Raising Self-Reliant Children in a Self-Indulgent World* by H. Stephen Glenn, Ph.D., and Jane Nelsen, Ed.D., copyright © 1989 by H. Stephen Glenn and Jane Nelsen. Used by permission of Prima Publishing, a member of the Crown Publishing Group, a division of Random House, Inc.

The quote on page 42 is from *Positive Discipline A–Z* by Jane Nelsen, Ed.D., Lynn Lott, M.A., M.F.C.C., and H. Stephen Glenn, Ph.D., copyright ©1999 by Jane Nelsen, Lynn Lott, and H. Stephen Glenn. Used by permission of Prima Publishing, a member of the Crown Publishing Group, a division of Random House, Inc.

The quotes on pages 52 and 82 are from *What Works with Children,* edited by Marshall P. Duke and Sara B. Duke, copyright © 2000. Used by permission of Peachtree Publishers.

The material on page 102 is adapted from *On Becoming Preteen Wise* by Gary Ezzo, M.A., and Robert Bucknam, M.D. (Simi Valley: Parent-Wise, 2000). Used by permission.

The quote on page 110 is from *The Shelter of Each Other* by Mary Pipher, Ph.D., copyright © 1996 by Mary Pipher, Ph.D. Used by permission of G.P. Putnam's Sons, a division of Penguin Putnam Inc.

Index compiled by Randl Ockey
Illustrations by Marieka Heinlen

10 9 8 7 6 5 4 3 2
Printed in Hong Kong

Free Spirit Publishing Inc.
217 Fifth Avenue North, Suite 200
Minneapolis, MN 55401-1299
(612) 338-2068
help4kids@freespirit.com
www.freespirit.com

The following are registered trademarks of Free Spirit Publishing Inc.:

FREE SPIRIT®
FREE SPIRIT PUBLISHING®
THE FREE SPIRITED CLASSROOM®

SELF-HELP FOR TEENS®
SELF-HELP FOR KIDS®
WORKS FOR KIDS®

HOW RUDE!™
LEARNING TO GET ALONG™
LAUGH & LEARN™

Dedication

To our families: Ed, Gus, and Rachel Hightower and Mark, Daniel and Mikey Riley. In loving rememberance of Russell Clay Johnson and Edward Augustus Hightower, Jr.

Acknowledgments

We'd like to thank our agents, Pamela Harty and Deidre Knight, who believed in our book from the start. (They are proof positive that you don't have to live in New York to be great agents!)

We both owe a great deal to Lee Walburn, long-time Editor-in-Chief of *Atlanta* Magazine, who has groomed and nurtured our careers for more than a decade.

Betsy would like to thank her parents, John and Jane Bell, for passing on the tradition of family devotionals.

Elaine is grateful for family members who are always there, offering support and encouragement: Dee Dee and Bill, Mimi, Linda, Scott, Christopher and Matthew, Brother Bill and Janet, Allan, Lolly, Savannah and Frank, Marti, Shelby and Kimzey, Tasha, Brian, Will and Annie, Eric, Alicia and Olivia; for friends near and far: Betty-Sue, Pam, Kris, Risa, Karen, Lee, Kristi, Carey, LeAnne, Tom and Jamie; and for our other "kids"—Weezie and Austin. A special thanks to Dr. Jim and Sandra Collins for their spiritual guidance and support. The Hightowers also have Mike McHugh to thank for suggesting we begin family meetings all those years ago. (To Mike: It worked!)

Contents

Weekly Meeting Agendas 7

Date Used	Title (Topic)	

Foreword

by Michele Borba, Ed.D.

A big part of our job as parents is the moral instruction of our children. It's up to us to teach them the values we want them to have—values that will guide them to make positive choices, avoid risky behaviors, and develop empathy, conscience, self-control, respect, kindness, tolerance, and fairness.

We can't assume that children will simply absorb these values on their own, as they go about their lives. In fact, we're right to be concerned about the negative influences with which they come into contact every day. Popular culture rarely encourages and often undermines moral character. Many G-rated movies flaunt disrespect for elders. Teen pop stars dress seductively and sing about surrendering to uncontrollable urges. Advertisements promote kids with "attitude" ranging from rude, sarcastic, and apathetic to overexcited, intense, and out of control.

If we as parents want our children to have solid character, or "moral intelligence," we must share with them why values matter—and listen to their inner struggles and questions.

With today's demanding schedules, finding quiet moments to discuss deeper issues is a challenge. It's not going to happen by accident. Parents must take the initiative and create opportunities to share values. One of the easiest ways to inspire such teachable moments is by holding family meetings.

Counselors have often recommended family meetings as a way to coordinate schedules, set goals, handle conflicts, and discuss values. But designing meaningful agendas can become a daunting, if not awkward, task for already overloaded parents. The beauty of the easy-to-use guide you're holding right now is that it requires no preparation. Families can sit down once a week, open the book, and share what's important to them.

Regardless of their personal priorities and beliefs, families of all types will relate to these topics. Elaine and Betsy present each subject in a way that prompts conversation without drawing conclusions. This open-ended style invites contributions from family members of all ages without "preaching" to kids. Children gain experience communicating with adults, while parents get to respond to and guide their children. Perhaps most importantly, during this time shared together, family members are able to devote their full attention to one another.

In a world of distractions and influences, "our full attention" is perhaps the greatest gift we can give our children.

Michele Borba, Ed.D., is the author of *Building Moral Intelligence: The Seven Essential Virtues that Teach Kids to Do the Right Thing* (San Francisco: Jossey-Bass, Wiley, 2001) and *Parents* Do *Make a Difference: How to Raise Kids with Solid Character, Strong Minds, and Caring Hearts* (San Francisco: Jossey-Bass, Wiley, 1999); *www.moralintelligence.com*.

Introduction

Why Your Family Needs Family Meetings

When we were children, families shared meal-times, leisurely summer evenings on the patio, weekly worship services, and long car trips to grandmother's house. Families didn't need meetings because they hashed out mutual concerns around the dinner table. But, with both parents working and children participating in more structured activities than ever before, hectic schedules are squeezing out the household rituals which bonded past generations. Togetherness is not something today's families can take for granted.

If we as parents want to pass on our values and raise strong, confident children, we have to be more deliberate about our parenting. Holding family meetings is one of the quickest, easiest ways to improve communication and build character within our families. These gatherings can require as little as 15 minutes each week, and *Our Family Meeting Book* makes planning the agendas simple and fun.

In a family meeting, everyone's opinion—even the youngest child's—is respected and heard.

Kids learn to assert themselves, communicate their feelings, listen to others' viewpoints, and solve problems. Everyone airs frustrations and shares dreams in a setting that is supportive and not emotionally charged. What's more, since every family member gets input into decision-making, they are more likely to embrace the resulting policies and expectations.

Family meetings also provide a practical way for families to coordinate busy schedules, distribute allowances, accomplish chores, plan menus, and more. You don't have to be organizationally challenged to be overwhelmed by today's hectic pace! Even a very organized parent will find family meetings helpful.

We're so convinced family meetings will become a treasured ritual for your family that we have designed *Our Family Meeting Book* to become a permanent keepsake. It will help you not only make memories, but preserve them for years to come.

How to Use This Book

Every family's meetings will be a little different, and *Our Family Meeting Book* is designed to be flexible.

There are 52 weekly agendas—one for each week of the year—but you don't have to use them in order. Use the Contents or Index to find a topic that speaks to the issues your family is dealing with right now. If certain agendas work very well for your family, feel free to repeat them. If others don't interest you, choose something else.

Each agenda has seven sections. Don't feel compelled to use every section every week, or to write something on every blank line. If a particular feature doesn't work for your family, skip it.

The sections are:

1. **Topic.** Each agenda starts with a read-aloud (or put-in-your-own-words) topic, plus a few "Let's Talk" questions for your family to discuss. If your family has prepared its own agenda, skip this section—or use both agendas.

2. **Accomplishments.** Don't just *praise* children, write it down! Years later, you'll enjoy this record of achievements both large and small.

3. **Expectations.** What are some of your goals, as a family and as individuals? Have you made any progress toward last week's goals?

4. **Family Matters.** Take a few notes about what you discuss or decide. This helps everyone remember what was said. During the week, you can use this space to jot down things you want to talk about at the next meeting.

5. **Parent-to-Parent.** This short bit of advice is aimed at you, the parents. It provides extra information or insight into the featured topic.

6. **Calendar.** This weekly planner helps you track and coordinate family activities.

7. **Menu Planner.** Tired of hearing complaints at mealtimes? Get the whole family involved in meal planning and preparation!

Starting on page 113, you'll also find a variety of helpful tools—forms and pages you can use to plan summer fun, family vacations, parties, and celebrations; manage allowances; and more. On pages 125–126, we've listed several resources (books, organizations, and Web sites) we know and recommend. You might consult some of these for more information on meeting agenda topics, or to get ideas for your own agendas. There's a wealth of parenting information out there, and we'll point you toward some of the best.

How to Hold a Family Meeting

Here are five basic elements of family meetings—although feel free to experiment with this formula. (Notice that the first letters of the key words spell out the acronym PEACE.)

- **Praise.** Begin your meeting by praising children for their accomplishments or positive attitudes. Although general compliments are always nice, try to recognize specific behaviors. For example, say, "I like the way you introduced yourself to Mrs. Phillips," instead of "I like it when you're friendly." If giving weekly compliments seems superficial to older teens, save the accolades for the big stuff. After you get the ball rolling, "open the floor" to anyone who wants to pay someone a compliment. Encourage siblings to commend each other, and teach children to say "thanks" for kind words.

- **Expectations.** This is a time to review chores and discuss problems completing assigned tasks. Again, be specific. ("Put the top on the toothpaste when you're finished," rather than "Keep the bathroom clean.") It's also an opportunity to teach your children how to set long- and short-term goals. For example, if a piano recital is coming up, encourage your child to memorize one page of music each week or practice five times daily. Children will be more likely to "buy into" these goals if they help set them.

- **Agenda.** During the week, any family member may jot down an issue he or she wishes to raise during the next meeting. This is the time to bring up family policies, negotiate disputes, set priorities, or plan future activities like vacations and summer camp—whatever your family needs to resolve that week. Regardless of whether your family has prepared its own agenda, *Our Family Meeting Book* provides a theme for you to read aloud and discuss.

- **Calendar.** Use this time to coordinate busy family schedules. Who's picking up who, when, and where?

- **Earnings.** End your family meeting by distributing allowances. If you hand out the money earlier, it will create a distraction. Also, the prospect of getting paid is sure to hold your

children's interest until the end. If your family doesn't use allowances, this final "E" can stand for "Ending." Wrap up your meeting with a prayer, song, or cheer—any positive affirmation of your family team!

Ten Tips for Holding a Successful Family Meeting

1. **Establish ground rules.** For example: Everyone gets a turn to talk without being interrupted. No TV, music, phone calls, toys, or hand-held video games during the meeting. Unless conflicts are unavoidable, all family members must be present (including teenagers).

2. **Have your meetings at the same time every week.** This helps family meetings become a habit and makes them easier to schedule. We find Sunday nights work best.

3. **Don't hesitate to call an emergency meeting.** When a crisis strikes, don't wait until your regularly scheduled date.

4. **Don't drag out meetings unnecessarily.** Fifteen minutes may be enough. But be flexible and follow your family's lead—some weeks may require more or less time.

5. **Review last week's goals.** Did you accomplish the goals you set last week? If not, what got in the way? What will you do to prevent roadblocks going forward?

6. **Give everyone a chance to participate.** Go around the table and ask for everyone's input, even the youngest child's. Start with the children so they're not unduly influenced by adult opinions.

7. **Allow the kids to moderate.** Once your family meetings are well established, let everyone, even the kids, take turns leading the meeting.

8. **Parents/guardians retain authority.** Although family meetings give children an opportunity to voice their opinions, final policy rulings are made by the parent or guardian.

9. **Include fun activities.** Try playing a game, telling a joke, creating something, sharing a story, singing a song.

10. **Conclude by holding hands.** Whether you yell a cheer, read an inspirational quotation, sing a song, say a prayer, or simply say what you're grateful for, take a moment to express family solidarity.

A Few Words About Families

These days, families come in many different forms. Yours may include biological or adoptive parents, single parents, stepparents, stepsiblings, legal guardians, unmarried partners, or other significant adults who live in your home and share in your family life in an important way. It may include foster children, grandchildren, nieces or nephews, cousins, or other relatives near or distant. Any household with an adult and a child can benefit from regular meetings, whether your family has two people or ten.

Although holding a "meeting" may seem unnecessary for a single parent and child, adults are often surprised at how much kids value this structure. The process gives children an opportunity to voice opinions and feel important. For adults, the meetings provide an opportunity to pass along expectations and values that might otherwise fall through the cracks.

If you're starting this tradition with older children, be prepared for a little resistance. You may have to adjust the "formula" slightly. Although teens may feel awkward at first, they'll soon find the meetings valuable—though don't expect them to tell you so. And don't be discouraged if you can't meet every week. Holding meetings as seldom as once a month can still make a big difference.

Weekly Meeting Agendas

WHAT DOES OUR FAMILY STAND FOR?

One good way to define family values is to create a family mission statement. Writing things down helps everyone recognize their true priorities. **Let's Talk:** How would we complete the following statements?

The most important thing our family believes in is . . .

The best part of being in our family is . . .

Our most important traditions are . . .

Together, we promise to strive for . . .

Accomplishments:

_____

_____

_____

_____

Expectations:

_____

_____

_____

Family Matters:

_____

_____

_____

_____

_____

_____

_____

_____

_____

_____

_____

GO PUBLIC!

FAMILY MISSION STATEMENT

Post your mission statement where visitors can see it (on the refrigerator, in the entryway, beside your children's artwork). Be proud of what you believe and what your family stands for!

Week of: __ / __ / __ Through: __ / __ / __

Menus

| **Monday** |
| A.M. | P.M. |

| **Tuesday** |
| A.M. | P.M. |

| **Wednesday** |
| A.M. | P.M. |

| **Thursday** |
| A.M. | P.M. |

| **Friday** |
| A.M. | P.M. |

| **Saturday** |
| A.M. | P.M. |

| **Sunday** |
| A.M. | P.M. |

"I HELP, TOO, DADDY"

Children as young as three can match socks and fold napkins. Grade schoolers can dust and clear the table. Older kids can vacuum and unload the dishwasher. There are many tasks kids can do alone or with a little help. **Let's Talk:** Does everyone in our family clean up his or her own messes? Does everyone know how to use the (safe) appliances? How is the workload distributed in our household? Is it a team effort? Is there anything we could do differently? **Tip:** Use the "Chore Chart" on page 123 to help you keep track of who does what in your home.

Accomplishments:
_____
_____
_____
_____

Expectations:
_____
_____
_____
_____

Family Matters:
_____
_____
_____
_____
_____
_____
_____
_____
_____

PARENT-TO-PARENT

"AND THE AWARD GOES TO. . ."

Allowing children to help out around the home is critical for developing a cooperative spirit. It reinforces children's sense of belonging and raises their self-esteem. Praise their efforts and find tangible ways to acknowledge your children's contributions. Reward them with stickers, small prizes, even a blue ribbon!

Week of: __ / __ / __ Through: __ / __ / __

Menus

Monday
A.M.   P.M.

Tuesday
A.M.   P.M.

Wednesday
A.M.   P.M.

Thursday
A.M.   P.M.

Friday
A.M.   P.M.

Saturday
A.M.   P.M.

Sunday
A.M.   P.M.

SHARE AND SHARE ALIKE

When a brother grabs a new toy or a sister gobbles the last piece of chocolate, it's hard to think about sharing. In her book *Building Moral Intelligence: The Seven Essential Virtues that Teach Kids to Do the Right Thing* (San Francisco: Jossey-Bass, Wiley, 2001), Michele Borba suggests that families can prevent such clashes by setting ground rules for sharing ahead of time. For example, if there's something you don't want to share with a friend, put it out of sight before the friend arrives. Anything within reach is fair game. **Let's Talk:** Is it okay not to share everything? When is it okay not to share? When is it important *to* share?

Accomplishments:

_____

_____

_____

Expectations:

_____

_____

_____

Family Matters:

_____

_____

_____

_____

_____

_____

_____

_____

PARENT-TO-PARENT

FAIR SHARES

Borba suggests three ways to help children learn to share:
1. Create sharing boundaries. (Allow children to say that some items are off-limits.)
2. Encourage sharing behaviors. (Praise your children when they do share.)
3. Emphasize the effect sharing has on others. (Motivate them to share by pointing out how good it makes others feel.)

Week of: __ / __ / __ Through: __ / __ / __   Menus

Monday

A.M.   P.M.

Tuesday

A.M.   P.M.

Wednesday

A.M.   P.M.

Thursday

A.M.   P.M.

Friday

A.M.   P.M.

Saturday

A.M.   P.M.

Sunday

A.M.   P.M.

MAKE A DATE

When is the last time our family went on a "date"? With today's busy schedules, it's easy to let regular commitments dominate our calendars. By the time we get a break, we're too exhausted to plan anything creative. You don't have to wait for a holiday or vacation to plan special outings. **Let's Talk:** Let's spend a few minutes brainstorming activities we enjoy doing together. Do we like building or creating something? Going on a hike or picnic? Attending a concert? Watching a ball game? Let's plan one special outing this month, or just start making a list of things we'd like to do. Then, when a free night pops up, we'll have plenty of ideas on hand. **Tip:** See "Free—or Nearly Free—Summer Activities" on page 115 for starter suggestions.

Accomplishments:

Expectations:

Family Matters:

ACQUIRED TASTES

One of the greatest legacies parents leave their children is the things they teach them to love. If you adore classic movies, chamber music, Mexican food, or ice hockey, chances are your kids love some or all of the same things. Think about the things you want your child to appreciate— are you making time to share your passion?

Week of: __ / __ / __ Through: __ / __ / __   Menus

Monday

A.M.   P.M.

Tuesday

A.M.   P.M.

Wednesday

A.M.   P.M.

Thursday

A.M.   P.M.

Friday

A.M.   P.M.

Saturday

A.M.   P.M.

Sunday

A.M.   P.M.

STRESSED TO IMPRESS

Today, three-year-olds are taking gymnastics, five-year-olds are joining soccer teams, seven-year-olds are studying drama, and young teens are studying for the SAT exam or working at part-time jobs. But is all this activity leaving families enriched or exhausted? **Let's Talk:** Are we stressing about things that aren't really important? Let's consider . . .

• Is it more satisfying to have lots of friends or lots of toys and clothes?

• For kids, does success mean winning at sports, getting the lead in the school play, making the Honor Roll, or something else? (What else?) What is the value of each?

• For adults, does success mean pursuing a career, buying a home, becoming a loving parent, or something else? (What else?) What is the value of each?

Does the way we spend our time and money reflect these choices?

Accomplishments:

_____

_____

_____

Expectations:

_____

_____

_____

Family Matters:

_____

_____

_____

_____

_____

_____

_____

PARENT·TO·PARENT

HYPER-PARENTING

In the book *The Over-Scheduled Child: Avoiding the Hyper-Parenting Trap* (New York: St. Martin's, 2001), Alvin Rosenfeld, M.D., and Nicole Wise contend that over-scheduling is not only stressful for parents but potentially harmful to kids. They write: "This life of pressure and perpetual motion . . . is giving us a generation-wide headache. It makes us feel tired and inadequate because no matter how much we have already done we could always be doing more."

Week of: __ / __ / __ Through: __ / __ / __   Menus

Monday

A.M.   P.M.

Tuesday

A.M.   P.M.

Wednesday

A.M.   P.M.

Thursday

A.M.   P.M.

Friday

A.M.   P.M.

Saturday

A.M.   P.M.

Sunday

A.M.   P.M.

WORD GAMES

Sometimes *how* something is said is more powerful than *what* is said. Think of how the meaning of these phrases could change with different tones of voice:

- "Are you wearing that to school?"
- "I don't feel like playing."
- "Who is he?" "Who is she?"
- "Where have you been?"

On the other hand, sometimes we hear "hidden messages" in other people's words, even when they didn't mean them at all. **Let's Talk:** Do misunderstandings like these ever happen in our family? What can we do to prevent them?

Accomplishments: _____
_____
_____
_____

Expectations: _____
_____
_____
_____

Family Matters: _____
_____
_____
_____
_____
_____
_____
_____

PARENT-TO-PARENT

WHAT'S THE DIFFERENCE?

"Don't forget your lunch money," versus "Remember to take your lunch money." The first sentence carries the *implication of failure,* while the second carries the *implication of responsibility.* It is a subtle but important difference. Think about how you phrase statements and what hidden meanings may go along with them.

Week of: __ / __ / __ Through: __ / __ / __   Menus

Monday

A.M.   P.M.

Tuesday

A.M.   P.M.

Wednesday

A.M.   P.M.

Thursday

A.M.   P.M.

Friday

A.M.   P.M.

Saturday

A.M.   P.M.

Sunday

A.M.   P.M.

RESPECT YOUR ELDERS

In many cultures, such as those in Africa and Asia, people have great respect for their elders. A traditional Ghanian proverb advises that because your parents took care of you while you were cutting your teeth, you should take care of them while they're losing theirs. In today's mobile society, young people are sometimes distant from older family members. Different generations may live hundreds or even thousands of miles apart. This makes it hard for kids to relate to older adults. **Let's Talk:** Why is it important to honor the elderly? Who are some of the older people our family knows? How can we show them special respect?

Accomplishments:

_____

_____

_____

Expectations:

_____

_____

_____

Family Matters:

_____

_____

_____

_____

_____

_____

_____

_____

_____

PARENT-TO-PARENT

ON THE RECORD

Have your child "interview" a grandparent or other older adult. Encourage him or her to ask simple questions like, "Where did you live when you were my age?" "What was your school like?" "What was your favorite food?" "Toy?" "How did you celebrate holidays?"

Week of: __ / __ / __ Through: __ / __ / __   Menus

Monday

A.M.   P.M.

Tuesday

A.M.   P.M.

Wednesday

A.M.   P.M.

Thursday

A.M.   P.M.

Friday

A.M.   P.M.

Saturday

A.M.   P.M.

Sunday

A.M.   P.M.

TEMPTING TAKEOVERS

Can a child learn to play an instrument only by watching someone else play? Can he or she learn to tie shoes only by watching Mom tie hers? How about writing book reports? Doing science projects? Sometimes it seems easier for parents to take over jobs their children need to do, usually to save time. But this makes things harder in the long run. Families need to build a little extra "learning time" into their schedules. **Let's Talk:** Do the kids in our family understand why the adults don't just do things for them? Is it ever okay for parents to take over? When?

Accomplishments:

_____

_____

_____

Expectations:

_____

_____

_____

Family Matters:

_____

_____

_____

_____

_____

_____

_____

_____

_____

PARENT-TO-PARENT

TO THE RESCUE

In their book *Raising Self-Reliant Children in a Self-Indulgent World* (Rocklin, CA: Prima Publishing, 2000), authors H. Stephen Glenn, Ph.D., and Jane Nelsen, Ed.D., write, "Too often as parents and teachers, we swoop in to rescue children instead of allowing them to experience the consequences of their behavior. Or we step in and explain things instead of helping them discover the meaning of an event for themselves."

Week of: __ / __ / __ Through: __ / __ / __   Menus

Monday

A.M.   P.M.

Tuesday

A.M.   P.M.

Wednesday

A.M.   P.M.

Thursday

A.M.   P.M.

Friday

A.M.   P.M.

Saturday

A.M.   P.M.

Sunday

A.M.   P.M.

FORGIVE AND FORGET

Mahatma Gandhi was a great leader who helped India win its independence from Great Britain. He insisted on nonviolent resistance, even when he was persecuted and imprisoned. Like Martin Luther King Jr., whose work he inspired, Gandhi was eventually assassinated by a person who disapproved of his tolerance for people who were different. One of the many inspiring things Gandhi said was: "The weak can never forgive. Forgiveness is the attribute of the strong." Today, popular movies, TV shows, video games, and books tend to show that revenge, not forgiveness, is the "attribute of the strong." **Let's Talk:** Which do you think takes more courage: forgiveness or revenge? Does forgiving someone mean you'll also forget what they did? Does it mean you'll never stand up for yourself? Are we holding any grudges against each other or someone outside our family? What needs to happen so we are ready to forgive?

Accomplishments:

_____

_____

_____

Expectations:

_____

_____

_____

Family Matters:

_____

_____

_____

_____

_____

PARENT-TO-PARENT

BULLY BUSTER

At some point in their lives, almost every child encounters a bully. If a peer is picking on your child, help him or her plan ways to avoid the antagonist. If confrontation is inevitable, teach your child to ignore the attack, to report the behavior to the proper authorities, or to be assertive without resorting to violence. Rehearse responses to common taunts. If you suspect that your child might be bullying others, talk with your child. Help your child learn to manage anger and resolve conflicts peacefully.

Week of: __ / __ / __ Through: __ / __ / __

Monday

A.M.   P.M.

Tuesday

A.M.   P.M.

Wednesday

A.M.   P.M.

Thursday

A.M.   P.M.

Friday

A.M.   P.M.

Saturday

A.M.   P.M.

Sunday

A.M.   P.M.

TRUE BLUE

After winning a big game or major award, sports heroes and movie stars always thank their "loyal fans." But what does it mean to be loyal to each other? **Let's Talk:** Here are some common dilemmas. What would a loyal person do in each circumstance?

- A person you want to impress says something negative and untrue about one of your friends.
- Your brother has a basketball game, but your favorite show is on TV. Do you go to his game or stay home?
- You signed up to participate in a car-wash fundraiser for your school; but when your alarm clock goes off on Saturday morning, you don't want to get out of bed.

Accomplishments:

_____

_____

_____

_____

Expectations:

_____

_____

_____

Family Matters:

_____

_____

_____

_____

_____

_____

_____

_____

_____

PARENT-TO-PARENT

COUNT ON ME

How well do you keep your own commitments? If your children see you "blowing off" appointments, practices, and other obligations, you can expect to see the same tendency in them.

Week of: __ / __ / __ Through: __ / __ / __   Menus

Monday

A.M.   P.M.

Tuesday

A.M.   P.M.

Wednesday

A.M.   P.M.

Thursday

A.M.   P.M.

Friday

A.M.   P.M.

Saturday

A.M.   P.M.

Sunday

A.M.   P.M.

JUST ONE OF THOSE DAYS

Do you ever have one of those days when things just go wrong from the start, and the day never gets any better? Maybe you spill your orange juice at breakfast. Then, at school, you fail a math test and don't get to be captain of the kickball team. After that, your best friend ignores you, and your favorite teacher tells you she's disappointed in you. Sometimes, even without things going wrong, we just feel down. Maybe we can't figure out what's bothering us, or we're anxious about something in the future. Maybe we have big worries—about parents or friends—or we're facing a tough situation like moving to a different town. At times like these, we have to call on our inner strength to make it through. **Let's Talk:** Where does our family get its inner strength?

Accomplishments:
_____
_____
_____
_____

Expectations:
_____
_____
_____

Family Matters:
_____
_____
_____
_____
_____
_____
_____
_____

PARENT-TO-PARENT

JUST TALKING TO MYSELF!

"HERE'S HOW I'LL MAKE MYSELF FEEL BETTER . . ."

Even if you don't realize it, you probably use positive self-talk to get through difficult times. This is a technique your children can use, too. For example: "I'm having a rotten day! Everybody is being mean to me. Maybe they'll be nicer tomorrow. I'll just keep myself company today. I'll get out my art supplies and listen to some music. That will make me feel better."

Week of: __ / __ / __ Through: __ / __ / __   Menus

Monday

A.M.   P.M.

Tuesday

A.M.   P.M.

Wednesday

A.M.   P.M.

Thursday

A.M.   P.M.

Friday

A.M.   P.M.

Saturday

A.M.   P.M.

Sunday

A.M.   P.M.

IT TAKES A COMMUNITY

"Community service" is just a fancy way of saying "helping out." It's really nothing new, because there have always been people willing to lend a hand. Without help from Sacagawea, Meriwether Lewis and William Clark would have never survived their famous journey across America. Think about the brave individuals who risked their lives helping slaves escape to freedom through the Underground Railroad. **Let's Talk:** Why do people use their time, energy, and resources to help others? Does our family help any community organizations or charities and why? What are some ways our family might choose to serve others?

Accomplishments:
_____
_____
_____
_____

Expectations:
_____
_____
_____
_____

Family Matters:
_____
_____
_____
_____
_____
_____
_____
_____
_____
_____

PARENT-TO-PARENT

KIDS CAN!

In her book, *The Kid's Guide to Service Projects* (Minneapolis: Free Spirit Publishing, 1995), Barbara A. Lewis describes many ways school-age kids can do service projects, both large and small. Younger children will enjoy sharing activities with their parents, such as assembling personal care kits (toothbrushes and toothpaste, combs, soap, shampoo, etc.) for families living in shelters. Older kids can organize environmental projects, like cleaning up their school grounds, planting a community garden, or helping at an animal shelter.

Week of: __ / __ / __ Through: __ / __ / __   Menus

Monday
A.M.   P.M.

Tuesday
A.M.   P.M.

Wednesday
A.M.   P.M.

Thursday
A.M.   P.M.

Friday
A.M.   P.M.

Saturday
A.M.   P.M.

Sunday
A.M.   P.M.

TAKE YOUR CHANCES

When children are roller-skating or learning to ride a bike, they often brag about who has fallen the least. But the kid who's fallen the *most* may be the one who's trying the hardest. Sometimes we play it *too* safe. If we never took a chance, we'd never learn to swim without floats. We'd never enter a contest or make new friends. One way family members can encourage each other to take smart risks is to give awards for bravery. For example, designate a special fancy dinner plate as the "brave plate" for recognizing feats of courage and other positive risk-taking action. **Let's Talk:** Let's each tell about a time when taking a risk paid off.

Accomplishments:

_____
_____
_____
_____

Expectations:

_____
_____
_____
_____

Family Matters:

_____
_____
_____
_____
_____
_____
_____
_____
_____

PARENT-TO-PARENT

LETTING GO

As our children's protector, it's hard to let them take risks, especially when we know they might fail. Consider the words of Florence Griffith Joyner, sprinter and three-time Olympic gold medalist: "You never fail until you stop trying."

Week of: __ / __ / __ Through: __ / __ / __   Menus

| Monday |
| A.M. | P.M. |

| Tuesday |
| A.M. | P.M. |

| Wednesday |
| A.M. | P.M. |

| Thursday |
| A.M. | P.M. |

| Friday |
| A.M. | P.M. |

| Saturday |
| A.M. | P.M. |

| Sunday |
| A.M. | P.M. |

PLAY FAIR!

"But it's not fair!" Every parent has heard that protest countless times. What does it really mean? It usually means that a child thinks another child is getting more than he or she is—more time, more money, more toys, more privileges. Little kids may think it's not fair *whenever* they don't get what they want. But as children grow up and mature, they learn to share and wait their turns. They learn that things won't always be *equal*. They also learn to compromise. **Let's Talk:** What is a compromise? How can compromises help us be fair to each other? Does being "fair" always mean being "equal"? When do we tend to complain about fairness? Are we really being unfair to each other? If so, how can we act more justly? Is it possible for things to be fair all the time?

Accomplishments:

_____

_____

_____

Expectations:

_____

_____

_____

Family Matters:

_____

_____

_____

_____

_____

_____

_____

_____

PARENT-TO-PARENT

UMPIRE, PLEASE!

In the book *Building Moral Intelligence: The Seven Essential Virtues that Teach Kids to Do the Right Thing* (San Francisco: Jossey-Bass, Wiley, 2001), Michele Borba suggests nine things to do when kids complain, "That's not fair!": 1) Calm everyone down, 2) Clarify feelings, 3) Let each child tell the story, 4) Don't take sides, 5) Make the kids part of the solution, 6) Don't let them get up until they solve the problem, 7) Ask kids to see it from the other side, 8) Offer a mediator, and 9) Find out the real cause.

Week of: __ / __ / __ Through: __ / __ / __   Menus

Monday

A.M.   P.M.

Tuesday

A.M.   P.M.

Wednesday

A.M.   P.M.

Thursday

A.M.   P.M.

Friday

A.M.   P.M.

Saturday

A.M.   P.M.

Sunday

A.M.   P.M.

LAUGH ATTACK

An Apache legend says that the Creator gave human beings (the "two-leggeds") the ability to do many things—talk, run, see, and hear. But he was not satisfied until they could do one more thing—laugh. And so the two-leggeds learned to laugh. Then the Creator said, "Now you are fit to live!" Sometimes the best way to deal with stressful situations is just to laugh, especially when we can laugh at ourselves. **Let's Talk:** Can we think of times when laughter helped us deal with difficult situations? If we were making a video of our family's funniest moments, what scenes would we include?

Accomplishments:

_____

_____

_____

_____

Expectations:

_____

_____

_____

_____

Family Matters:

_____

_____

_____

_____

_____

_____

_____

_____

_____

_____

_____

FUNNY BONES

TICKLE TIME 2:00!

Make time for laughter. Read aloud humorous books to your kids, rent funny movies, and start a collection of jokes and riddles. Have a good humor bulletin board, which can include items such as favorite comic strips from the newspaper.

Week of: __ / __ / __ Through: __ / __ / __   Menus

Monday

A.M.   P.M.

Tuesday

A.M.   P.M.

Wednesday

A.M.   P.M.

Thursday

A.M.   P.M.

Friday

A.M.   P.M.

Saturday

A.M.   P.M.

Sunday

A.M.   P.M.

BE PREPARED!

The famous Boy Scout motto is "Be prepared." When disaster strikes, being prepared can mean the difference between life and death. The American Red Cross urges families to arrange a "Family Disaster Plan," which outlines what to do in case of emergency. For example, everyone should know when and how to evacuate the house (and what to do about pets). In the middle of a crisis, it's hard to think clearly. A little forethought and trial runs help keep everyone safe. **Let's Talk:** What types of disasters are most likely to happen where we live? (Severe weather, natural disasters, auto accidents, fire, injury, crime?) What should we do if any of these things occur? Who should we call for help, and where are their phone numbers? Where are our emergency supplies?

Accomplishments:

_____
_____
_____
_____

Expectations:

_____
_____
_____
_____

Family Matters:

_____
_____
_____
_____
_____
_____
_____
_____

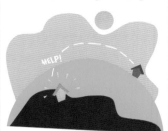

PARENT-TO-PARENT

CREATE A CONTACT

Establish a family member or friend who lives in another town or state as a contact person in case of an emergency. This person would likely live out of the danger zone and can help you keep track of everyone's location. For more tips on disaster preparedness, contact the Federal Emergency Management Agency (FEMA) at 1-800-480-2520, or write to them at 500 C Street SW, Washington, DC 20472. See their Web site at *www.fema.gov*.

Week of: __ / __ / __ Through: __ / __ / __

Menus

Monday

A.M.   P.M.

Tuesday

A.M.   P.M.

Wednesday

A.M.   P.M.

Thursday

A.M.   P.M.

Friday

A.M.   P.M.

Saturday

A.M.   P.M.

Sunday

A.M.   P.M.

TOO MUCH OF A GOOD THING

With so much publicity about people who don't have "enough"—food, medicine, clothing, shelter—it seems absurd to suggest that those who have "too much" may also suffer. But that's what Dan Kindlon, Ph.D., suggests in his book *Too Much of a Good Thing: Raising Children of Character in an Indulgent Age* (New York: Hyperion, 2001). He writes: "We give our kids too much and demand too little of them." Kindlon believes that children in an affluent society don't get enough opportunities to "struggle." **Let's Talk:** If someone says you did a good job but you know you didn't really try hard, how does it make you feel? Which makes you feel better about yourself—struggling to accomplish something and succeeding, or doing something easily?

Accomplishments:

_____

_____

_____

Expectations:

_____

_____

_____

Family Matters:

_____

_____

_____

_____

_____

_____

_____

_____

PARENT·TO·PARENT

WHEN I WAS YOUR AGE...

Children groan when their parents start the familiar refrain, "When I was your age, we didn't have . . ." They may never believe you were a deprived child (and, after all, you might not have been), but it's still inspiring for children to hear stories of how previous generations faced obstacles and overcame them.

Week of: __ / __ / __ Through: __ / __ / __

Menus

Monday
A.M.   P.M.

Tuesday
A.M.   P.M.

Wednesday
A.M.   P.M.

Thursday
A.M.   P.M.

Friday
A.M.   P.M.

Saturday
A.M.   P.M.

Sunday
A.M.   P.M.

OUT OF BOUNDS

Can you imagine trying to play a card game without rules? Or making up rules as you go along? It would cause confusion and perhaps arguments. Yet many families constantly negotiate and re-negotiate procedures for doing chores, going to bed, snacking, spending allowances, inviting friends over, watching television, or doing homework. It's exhausting for parents and children alike. **Let's Talk:** What are the five most important rules in our family? Would it help to post them on the refrigerator?

Accomplishments:

_____

_____

_____

_____

Expectations:

_____

_____

_____

_____

Family Matters:

_____

_____

_____

_____

_____

_____

_____

_____

_____

_____

_____

PARENT·TO·PARENT

ROUTINES RULE

A.M. SCHEDULE
8:00 – WAKE UP!
8:15 – BREAKFAST
8:30 – SHOWER/DRESS
8:45 – FEED GOLDFISH
9:00 – CATCH THE BUS

"Children enjoy routines and respond favorably to them," note Jane Nelsen, Ed.D., Lynn Lott, M.A., M.F.C.C., and H. Stephen Glenn, Ph.D., in their book *Positive Discipline A–Z* (Rocklin, CA: Prima Publishing, 2000). "Once routines are in place, the routine is the boss and the parent doesn't have to give orders continually." What a relief!

Week of: __ / __ / __ Through: __ / __ / __

Menus

Monday
A.M.   P.M.

Tuesday
A.M.   P.M.

Wednesday
A.M.   P.M.

Thursday
A.M.   P.M.

Friday
A.M.   P.M.

Saturday
A.M.   P.M.

Sunday
A.M.   P.M.

COMEBACK LINES

Since teenagers were invented, parents have been hearing, "But everybody's doing it. . . . " *Everybody* listens to that music, wears those clothes, goes to that movie, and so on. Truth is, everybody is probably *not* doing it. But more importantly, people of all ages must learn to resist peer pressure. Even young children must learn to say "no" when their friends run into the street or "borrow" someone else's toys without asking. One of the best ways to handle peer pressure is with humor. For example, if a friend tries to get you to shoplift some candy, you could say, "Are you kidding? I've got such bad luck I can't steal a cookie without my mom catching me in the act." **Let's Talk:** Are any of us having a tough time with peer pressure? Let's help each other think of some good "comeback lines."

Accomplishments:

_____

_____

_____

_____

Expectations:

_____

_____

_____

Family Matters:

_____

_____

_____

_____

_____

_____

_____

_____

PARENT-TO-PARENT

PASSING FAD

Every holiday season, there are news stories about parents who go to great lengths to buy their kids the year's hottest toys. Although some special toys are worth the effort, others are popular simply *because* everybody wants them. Think about whether you should encourage your child's desire to have the latest gizmo or resist going along with the fad.

Week of: __ / __ / __ Through: __ / __ / __

Menus

Monday
A.M.

P.M.

Tuesday
A.M.

P.M.

Wednesday
A.M.

P.M.

Thursday
A.M.

P.M.

Friday
A.M.

P.M.

Saturday
A.M.

P.M.

Sunday
A.M.

P.M.

CHEATERS NEVER WIN

Surveys show that more students and adults are cheating than ever—on exams, on tax forms, on their expense reports at work, and more. What's even more alarming is that many of them don't consider their actions wrong. **Let's Talk:** Does "anything go" as long as you don't get caught? Consider the following situations, and discuss whether the person is cheating:

- Tyson's test paper slips to the floor. Susie picks it up and hands it to him, but she happens to notice some of his answers are different than hers. Tyson is the best student in the class, so Susie quickly changes her answers.

- Jeff and Thanh are best friends, and they like to do their homework together. The teacher never asked them to work alone, so they usually share all their answers.

- Angela is playing center field for her softball team. The batter hits a long fly ball into the outfield, and Angela dives for it. Although the ball hits the ground, she scoops it up and pretends she made the catch. The umpire calls the batter out.

In the short run, it often appears that cheaters do win, but what are some reasons why they lose in the long run?

Accomplishments:

_____

_____

_____

Expectations:

_____

_____

_____

Family Matters:

_____

_____

_____

_____

WHITE LIES

CAUTION

As adults, we understand that all rules were not created equal. Cheating on your income tax is hardly the same as driving five miles over the speed limit. Most of us have told "white lies" to avoid hurting someone's feelings. But children see things in black and white. It's important to set a positive example.

Week of: __ / __ / __ Through: __ / __ / __

Menus

Monday	
A.M.	P.M.

Tuesday	
A.M.	P.M.

Wednesday	
A.M.	P.M.

Thursday	
A.M.	P.M.

Friday	
A.M.	P.M.

Saturday	
A.M.	P.M.

Sunday	
A.M.	P.M.

YOU DON'T HAVE TO SHOUT

With all the voices blaring on TV, in movies, and on the radio, sometimes it seems like we have to shout to be heard. Although yelling can release tension, it's rarely an effective way to communicate with each other. **Let's Talk:** Would any of the following ideas help control the noise level in our home?

- Make a list of "quiet" places, "loud" places, and those in between. Why is it okay to yell on the playground but not in the library?

- Agree on a family signal that means "lower your voice." (Whispering to children can be an inconspicuous signal that they are getting too loud.)

- Make it a family habit to say "Excuse me" or "May I have your attention?" when you need someone else to listen to you.

- Designate a "quiet time" each evening for reading or individual projects.

- Discuss individual tolerances for noises like stereo or TV volume and how to accommodate one another.

Accomplishments:

_____

_____

_____

_____

Expectations:

_____

_____

_____

_____

Family Matters:

_____

_____

_____

_____

_____

_____

_____

PARENT-TO-PARENT

LISTEN UP

Children don't always pick the best times to talk. Sometimes you have to ask them to wait until you can listen. Speak with your kids about the best times for them to get your attention, and vice versa. Remind them of this when they demand your attention at an inappropriate time.

Week of: __ / __ / __ Through: __ / __ / __

Menus

Monday

A.M.   P.M.

Tuesday

A.M.   P.M.

Wednesday

A.M.   P.M.

Thursday

A.M.   P.M.

Friday

A.M.   P.M.

Saturday

A.M.   P.M.

Sunday

A.M.   P.M.

DRESS CODE

What we wear has a lot to say about who we are. Wearing the "right" clothes can create confidence, but it's easy to get too caught up in appearances. **Let's Talk:** Take turns finishing the sentence, "If I had my choice, I would wear _____ every day!" How different are we? Which has the most influence on our preferences—comfort, style, or some other factor? Can you think of an experience where wearing something inappropriate or different caused you to feel out of place? How important is it to dress a certain way? How important is it to wear what our friends are wearing?

Accomplishments:

_____

_____

_____

_____

Expectations:

_____

_____

_____

Family Matters:

_____

_____

_____

_____

_____

_____

_____

_____

_____

_____

_____

GRIN AND LET THEM WEAR IT

As children begin to develop their own sense of style, you may be startled by their choices. Maybe it's time to drag out the yearbook and refresh your memory about some of *your* early choices! Set limits about what you consider inappropriate (such as provocative clothing), then let them decide.

Week of: __ / __ / __ Through: __ / __ / __

Monday
A.M.

P.M.

Tuesday
A.M.

P.M.

Wednesday
A.M.

P.M.

Thursday
A.M.

P.M.

Friday
A.M.

P.M.

Saturday
A.M.

P.M.

Sunday
A.M.

P.M.

NEVER GIVE UP

Former U.S. President Calvin Coolidge wrote, "Nothing in this world can take the place of persistence. Talent will not; nothing is more common than unsuccessful people with talent. Genius will not; unrewarded genius is almost a proverb. Education will not; the world is full of educated derelicts. Persistence and determination alone are omnipotent. The slogan 'press on' has solved and always will solve the problems of the human race." What does this mean? It means, "Never give up." **Let's Talk:** Can you think of a time when you succeeded *not* because you were the *best* but because you tried the *hardest?*

Accomplishments:

_____

_____

_____

Expectations:

_____

_____

_____

Family Matters:

_____

_____

_____

_____

_____

_____

_____

_____

I THINK I CAN

If you haven't already, make reading the children's story *The Little Engine That Could* (New York: Platt & Munk, 1954) a regular part of your child's bedtime routine. In this classic tale, the Little Engine succeeds in doing the impossible. In his book *What Works with Children* (Atlanta: Peachtree, 2000), child psychologist Marshall P. Duke writes, "The single most powerful source of self-esteem—for children and adults—is doing something you thought you could not do and doing it pretty well in your own eyes."

Week of: __ / __ / __ Through: __ / __ / __   Menus

Monday

A.M.   P.M.

Tuesday

A.M.   P.M.

Wednesday

A.M.   P.M.

Thursday

A.M.   P.M.

Friday

A.M.   P.M.

Saturday

A.M.   P.M.

Sunday

A.M.   P.M.

FULL ESTEEM AHEAD

Every family member has different gifts. Dad might have a great singing voice, Mom might be very athletic, and the oldest child might be a math whiz. But nobody is good at everything. Recognizing our unique strengths helps us feel good about ourselves. It also gives us the confidence to try new things, and even to make mistakes. **Let's Talk:** Let's name three great things about each member of our family.

Accomplishments:

_____

_____

_____

_____

Expectations:

_____

_____

_____

_____

Family Matters:

_____

_____

_____

_____

_____

_____

_____

_____

_____

_____

_____

FINDING THE WORDS

THANK YOU

It's easy to recognize a child who's smart, naturally athletic, or handsome. But people can have many talents and different ways of being smart. Look for creative opportunities to praise your child, especially for abilities the child has *earned* rather than *inherited*. For example, is your child *diligent* about finishing tasks, and therefore accomplished . . . *responsible* about pets (you don't have to remind him or her to walk the dog) . . . *thoughtful* when he or she makes cards for friends or relatives. . . .

Week of: __ / __ / __ Through: __ / __ / __   Menus

Monday
A.M.   P.M.

Tuesday
A.M.   P.M.

Wednesday
A.M.   P.M.

Thursday
A.M.   P.M.

Friday
A.M.   P.M.

Saturday
A.M.   P.M.

Sunday
A.M.   P.M.

DREAM TEAM

Few children grow up to be professional athletes, but many families place a high value on participating in team sports. Why? Kids may be surprised to learn that grown-ups in almost every profession rely on teamwork to succeed. Just like in sports, an office has coworkers who "hog the ball," break the rules, or don't pay attention. Rarely do we get to be part of a "dream team"—in sports or real life. Nevertheless, being part of a team helps us accomplish things we couldn't do as individuals. **Let's Talk:** What are some benefits of being on a team? Have you ever been on a special team? What made it so great? How is our family like a team? What can we do to improve our teamwork?

Accomplishments:

_____
_____
_____
_____

Expectations:

_____
_____
_____

Family Matters:

_____
_____
_____
_____
_____
_____
_____
_____
_____

PARENT·TO·PARENT

WHAT'S YOUR POSITION?

Explain to children how a baseball team needs more than one great player to craft a winning season. Likewise, your family needs every member's contribution to run smoothly. Discuss various family roles and how they're important and valuable. Praise children for their unique contributions to the game plan.

Week of: __ / __ / __ Through: __ / __ / __   Menus

Monday

A.M.   P.M.

Tuesday

A.M.   P.M.

Wednesday

A.M.   P.M.

Thursday

A.M.   P.M.

Friday

A.M.   P.M.

Saturday

A.M.   P.M.

Sunday

A.M.   P.M.

FOUL!

Families have different tolerances for cursing. Although some words are clearly inappropriate, words or phrases like "shut up" may be okay in one family but forbidden in another. According to the Parents Television Council, an advocacy group based in Los Angeles (707 Wilshire Boulevard, #2075, Los Angeles, CA 90017; 1-800-882-6868; *www.parentstv.org*), prime-time television profanity increased over 500 percent from 1989 to 1999. Adults and children alike tend to speak what they hear. **Let's Talk:** What words does our family disapprove of? Why? Should children and adults abide by the same rules about what's okay and not okay to say? Why do people use foul language in the first place?

Accomplishments:

Expectations:

Family Matters:

PARENT-TO-PARENT

THE 3 Rs

REASON
+ RESPECT
+ RESPONSIBILITY
= RIGHT!

Tim Jay, author of *What to Do When Your Kids Talk Dirty* (San Jose, CA: Resource Publications, 1997), urges parents to advocate the three Rs—reason, respect, and responsibility. Children (and adults) should think before they speak and be considerate of their audience. What may be acceptable around friends is not necessarily appropriate when grandmother is visiting!

Week of: __ / __ / __ Through: __ / __ / __   Menus

Monday

A.M.   P.M.

Tuesday

A.M.   P.M.

Wednesday

A.M.   P.M.

Thursday

A.M.   P.M.

Friday

A.M.   P.M.

Saturday

A.M.   P.M.

Sunday

A.M.   P.M.

MUM'S THE WORD

Can you keep a secret? Respecting a confidence demonstrates loyalty and trustworthiness. It takes maturity to resist the thrill of "telling." **Let's Talk:** Has anyone ever blabbed one of your secrets? How did it make you feel? When is it *not* okay to keep a secret? There are times when it's more important to "tell" than it is to keep silent, especially when someone's safety is at stake. In those times, does telling make you a tattletale? Why or why not?

Accomplishments:

Expectations:

Family Matters:

PRIVACY, PLEASE

PLEASE KNOCK BEFORE ENTERING!

Treat your children's requests for privacy as seriously as you would those of a peer. If there is no legitimate reason to tell another person what was revealed to you in confidence, don't break that trust simply because the matter seems insignificant by adult standards.

Week of: __ / __ / __ Through: __ / __ / __

Menus

Monday

A.M.

P.M.

Tuesday

A.M.

P.M.

Wednesday

A.M.

P.M.

Thursday

A.M.

P.M.

Friday

A.M.

P.M.

Saturday

A.M.

P.M.

Sunday

A.M.

P.M.

NEVER SAY NEVER

If you hear statements like, "You are *always* late!" or "You *never* clean up your room!" (or share your toys, or finish your homework, or hang up your towel), do you feel encouraged to do better next time? You might think, "What's the use of trying?" Words like "always" and "never" can do more harm than good. After all, few people make mistakes every time. **Let's Talk:** Do "always" and "never" crop up in our family conversations? Instead of saying, "You *never* get to bed on time!" or "You *never* let me do what I want to do!" what are some more constructive ways we can talk about problems or concerns?

Accomplishments:

_____

_____

_____

_____

Expectations:

_____

_____

_____

_____

Family Matters:

_____

_____

_____

_____

_____

_____

_____

_____

_____

ALWAYS THE CRITIC!

Criticism rarely motivates anyone. You can be clear with children about their responsibilities without attacking their characters. Compare the meaning of "You're such a slob. Why don't you ever make your bed?" with "Isn't it your responsibility to make your bed each day?"

Week of: __ / __ / __ Through: __ / __ / __   Menus

Monday

A.M.   P.M.

Tuesday

A.M.   P.M.

Wednesday

A.M.   P.M.

Thursday

A.M.   P.M.

Friday

A.M.   P.M.

Saturday

A.M.   P.M.

Sunday

A.M.   P.M.

BOREDOM BUSTERS

Families portrayed in television programs always have some dramatic episode unfolding in their lives. Cartoons entertain and tantalize viewers with continuous surprises. Between shows, exciting MTV-style commercials explode before us, touting the super-fantastic taste of neon-colored cereal. This can make real life seem awfully tedious, but boredom is a natural part of growing up. Boredom prompts us to use our imaginations and develop our natural interests. **Let's Talk:** Can boredom be a good thing? What are some things you can do when you're bored? **Tip:** Check out "Free—or Nearly Free—Summer Activities" on page 115 for some boredom-busting ideas. Many are doable year-round.

Accomplishments: _____

_____

_____

_____

Expectations: _____

_____

_____

_____

Family Matters: _____

_____

_____

_____

_____

_____

_____

_____

_____

_____

PARENT-TO-PARENT

SET THE STAGE

Resist "saving" your children from boredom. Insist that they forego outside distractions, such as the television, for at least part of the day or week. Children must learn to tune in to their inner selves for "entertainment," just as you do. Give them this opportunity.

Week of: __ / __ / __ Through: __ / __ / __

Menus

Monday		
A.M.	P.M.	

Tuesday		
A.M.	P.M.	

Wednesday		
A.M.	P.M.	

Thursday		
A.M.	P.M.	

Friday		
A.M.	P.M.	

Saturday		
A.M.	P.M.	

Sunday		
A.M.	P.M.	

DON'T TALK TO STRANGERS

A common compliment for a friendly person is, "He or she never met a stranger." But sometimes it's hard to know who's a stranger and who's not. What about a friend's dad whom you've never met? The telephone repair person? An unfamiliar teacher? **Let's Talk:** Why can it be dangerous to talk to strangers? Does that mean we should never be friendly to people we don't know? How can we be friendly and safe at the same time?

Accomplishments:

_____

_____

_____

_____

Expectations:

_____

_____

_____

_____

Family Matters:

_____

_____

_____

_____

_____

_____

_____

_____

_____

_____

_____

_____

_____

PARENT-TO-PARENT

PASSWORD, PLEASE

FROG!

RIGHT!

Come up with a family password—the sillier the better (easy to remember!). Then, if you ever have a sudden change of plans and have to send someone unexpected to pick up your child, give that person the password. This lets your child know that you really sent the messenger. Check periodically to make sure everyone remembers the password.

Week of: __ / __ / __ Through: __ / __ / __   Menus

Monday
A.M.   P.M.

Tuesday
A.M.   P.M.

Wednesday
A.M.   P.M.

Thursday
A.M.   P.M.

Friday
A.M.   P.M.

Saturday
A.M.   P.M.

Sunday
A.M.   P.M.

NO IFS, ANDS, OR BUTS!

Do you find it hard to give a compliment without tacking on a little instructional "advice"? Are you tempted to say, "Good work, but ..." and then go on to describe how it could have been better? When someone does this, it can take the impact out of the compliment. **Let's Talk:** Can we think of examples in our own experience when praise has been overshadowed by criticism? Next time we offer congratulations, let's remember, "No buts allowed!"

Accomplishments:

_____

_____

_____

_____

Expectations:

_____

_____

_____

_____

Family Matters:

_____

_____

_____

_____

_____

_____

_____

_____

_____

SAVE IT!

Does "no buts allowed" mean that parents aren't supposed to point out areas where children need to improve? No! In their book *Raising Self-Reliant Children in a Self-Indulgent World* (Rocklin, CA: Prima Publishing, 2000), H. Stephen Glenn, Ph.D., and Jane Nelsen, Ed.D., urge parents to make corrections a "separate transaction" at a later time. They advise, "Let the celebration of an improvement stand alone."

Week of: __ / __ / __ Through: __ / __ / __   Menus

Monday

A.M.   P.M.

Tuesday

A.M.   P.M.

Wednesday

A.M.   P.M.

Thursday

A.M.   P.M.

Friday

A.M.   P.M.

Saturday

A.M.   P.M.

Sunday

A.M.   P.M.

MAGIC WORDS

Back in 1969, manners expert Elizabeth L. Post wrote, "Etiquette was never intended to be a rigid set of rules. It is, rather, a code of behavior that is based on consideration, kindness, and unselfishness—something that should not, and will not, ever change." Good manners are less about writing proper thank-you notes than letting people know you received their gifts and are grateful. It's more important to let someone know you care than to use the "right" words. **Let's Talk:** Why are good manners important? Do the children in our home routinely use "magic words" like "please" and "thank you"? How about the adults? What are three or four areas where we could use some improvement? Would it be fun to give a weekly good manners award?

Accomplishments:

_____

_____

_____

_____

Expectations:

_____

_____

_____

Family Matters:

_____

_____

_____

_____

_____

_____

_____

_____

GLAD TO MEET YOU!

Children who are seen and not heard will return the favor. If you want your child to be cordial toward other adults, the best way is to pay attention to your child. Kids need to believe that grown-ups care about what they have to say and that adults respect them.

Week of: __ / __ / __ Through: __ / __ / __   Menus

Monday	
A.M.	P.M.

Tuesday	
A.M.	P.M.

Wednesday	
A.M.	P.M.

Thursday	
A.M.	P.M.

Friday	
A.M.	P.M.

Saturday	
A.M.	P.M.

Sunday	
A.M.	P.M.

FROM "ME" TO "WE"

In his book, *The 7 Habits of Highly Effective Families* (New York: St. Martin's Griffin, 1998), author Stephen R. Covey encourages family members to be loyal to each other—even to those who are not present. **Let's Talk:** What are some ways family members might be "disloyal" to each other? Is it disloyal to share a sibling's secret with your friends? To say mean things about each other? Such behavior hurts feelings and breaks down family trust. Covey goes on to say, "The way you treat any relationship in the family will eventually affect every relationship in the family." Can we make the decision to be an "all for one and one for all" type of family?

Accomplishments:

_____

_____

_____

Expectations:

_____

_____

_____

Family Matters:

_____

_____

_____

_____

_____

_____

_____

_____

_____

_____

PARENT-TO-PARENT

THE MISSING PIECE

Covey says that families need a clear vision for their family "culture." This vision should be an outlook that everybody helps to form, or at least understands. He says, "Have you ever done a jigsaw puzzle or seen someone doing one? How important is it that all who are working on it have the same final scene in mind?"

Week of: __ / __ / __ Through: __ / __ / __   Menus

Monday	
A.M.	P.M.

Tuesday	
A.M.	P.M.

Wednesday	
A.M.	P.M.

Thursday	
A.M.	P.M.

Friday	
A.M.	P.M.

Saturday	
A.M.	P.M.

Sunday	
A.M.	P.M.

HOME ALONE

On TV, kids rule the roost. In fact (as in the *Home Alone* movie series), parents are sometimes portrayed as bumbling idiots who can't keep up with their children! Experts often advise that kids under age 12 are better off with adult supervision whenever possible. **Let's Talk:** When children are old enough to be responsible for themselves for a short time, what are some reasonable ground rules? For example, is it okay to invite friends over? To use the oven? To answer the front door?

Accomplishments:

Expectations:

Family Matters:

PARENT-TO-PARENT

TEEN IDLE

RRRRRRRRRiiing!

In 2001, the YMCA commissioned a survey to learn what teens do after school. Teens who are supervised every day were compared with those who are unsupervised one or more days a week. According to the survey, unsupervised teens are more likely to:

- drink alcohol (34 vs. 22 percent)
- smoke cigarettes (16 vs. 11 percent)
- engage in sex (17 vs. 11 percent)
- use marijuana or other drugs (14 vs. 4 percent)
- skip a day of school (27 vs. 14 percent)
- skip classes at school (30 vs. 11 percent)

Source: U.S. Department of Justice, Office of Juvenile Justice and Delinquency Prevention, *OJJDP Fact Sheet*, May 2001, #14, "The YMCA's Teen Action Agenda."

Week of: __ / __ / __   Through: __ / __ / __

Menus

Monday

A.M.   P.M.

Tuesday

A.M.   P.M.

Wednesday

A.M.   P.M.

Thursday

A.M.   P.M.

Friday

A.M.   P.M.

Saturday

A.M.   P.M.

Sunday

A.M.   P.M.

BENDING THE RULES

All rules aren't created equal. Wearing a baseball cap forward rather than backward is not as important as looking both ways before crossing the street. Sometimes, families waste too much energy arguing over minor issues. It's hard for parents to enforce a rule when even they have begun to wonder if it is necessary. **Let's Talk:** What rules does our family fight about the most? Which ones are most important? Why? Are there any that might need to be updated or tossed out?

Accomplishments:

_____
_____
_____

Expectations:

_____
_____
_____

Family Matters:

_____
_____
_____
_____
_____
_____
_____
_____

MAJOR ON THE MAJORS

Mom & DAD'S TOOLS and RULES

According to Jody Johnston Pawel, author of *The Parent's Toolshop* (Springboro, OH: Ambris Publishing, 2000), "When parents say no too often, they end up with kids who constantly test limits, or who become sneaky to get around what they see as unreasonable rules."

Week of: __ / __ / __ Through: __ / __ / __

Menus

Monday

A.M.

P.M.

Tuesday

A.M.

P.M.

Wednesday

A.M.

P.M.

Thursday

A.M.

P.M.

Friday

A.M.

P.M.

Saturday

A.M.

P.M.

Sunday

A.M.

P.M.

THE ELEPHANT MAN

A 1980 movie telling the true story of an English boy born in the mid-1800s opened many people's eyes to the dangers of prejudice. The boy, John Merrick, suffered from a disease that so disfigured his skin and the shape of his head that people called him the "Elephant Man." A kind doctor rescued John from his life as a sideshow attraction, where people labeled him a "freak," and found a safe place for him to live. Inside his heart, John was the same as anyone else, and he needed the companionship and love that we all crave. **Let's Talk:** What does *The Elephant Man* teach us about tolerance for people who are not the same as us? In what ways may people be different or act differently than us? In what ways can we treat them with compassion and tolerance?

Accomplishments:

_____

_____

_____

Expectations:

_____

_____

_____

Family Matters:

_____

_____

_____

_____

_____

_____

_____

Week of: __ / __ / __   Through: __ / __ / __   Menus

Monday

A.M.   P.M.

Tuesday

A.M.   P.M.

Wednesday

A.M.   P.M.

Thursday

A.M.   P.M.

Friday

A.M.   P.M.

Saturday

A.M.   P.M.

Sunday

A.M.   P.M.

FOODIES

Young children are notoriously picky eaters. Some kids eat only hot dogs and applesauce or chicken fingers and French fries. Poor eating habits are not only unhealthy but wasteful. **Let's Talk:** Does our family throw away too much food? What are some ways we could improve our eating habits? Let's brainstorm some healthy snacks and dinner menus that everyone would enjoy.

Accomplishments:

_____

_____

_____

_____

Expectations:

_____

_____

_____

_____

Family Matters:

_____

_____

_____

_____

_____

_____

_____

_____

_____

_____

PARENT-TO-PARENT

FOOD FIGHT

As preteens and teens begin to assert their independence, food often becomes a way to proclaim, "I'm not you!" Try enlisting your independent child's creativity in the kitchen. Making food planning and preparation a regular part of shared family activity is one way to support your child's growing sense of independence. It also takes some of the "what's for dinner?" burden off of you.

Week of: __ / __ / __ Through: __ / __ / __   Menus

Monday

A.M.   P.M.

Tuesday

A.M.   P.M.

Wednesday

A.M.   P.M.

Thursday

A.M.   P.M.

Friday

A.M.   P.M.

Saturday

A.M.   P.M.

Sunday

A.M.   P.M.

BOASTING RIGHT

What's the difference between being conceited and being confident? Between bragging and being assertive? Sometimes there's a fine line between being stuck-up and being self-assured. Everyone knows somebody who likes to tell you how great she or he is. It's easy to see why that gets on your nerves. On the other hand, if you don't believe in yourself enough, people can take advantage of you. **Let's Talk:** What is bragging? Why is it wrong to brag? Can you express confidence without bragging? How?

Accomplishments:

_____
_____
_____

Expectations:

_____
_____
_____

Family Matters:

_____
_____
_____
_____
_____
_____
_____
_____
_____

PARENT-TO-PARENT

CAN DO

In the book *What Works with Children*, edited by Marshall P. Duke and Sara B. Duke (Atlanta, GA: Peachtree, 2000), long-time educator Ron Luckie advises, "Helping your child acquire confidence is more important than teaching your child competence. The world is full of competent people who are able to accomplish little because they lack confidence. Confident people find a way to be competent."

Week of: __ / __ / __ Through: __ / __ / __   Menus

Monday
A.M.   P.M.

Tuesday
A.M.   P.M.

Wednesday
A.M.   P.M.

Thursday
A.M.   P.M.

Friday
A.M.   P.M.

Saturday
A.M.   P.M.

Sunday
A.M.   P.M.

SWEET DREAMS

Ancient Egyptians relied on their dreams to help them make important political decisions. The ancient Chinese believed that each person had two souls, one connected to the body and the other to the spirit. The spiritual soul was revealed in sleep and dreams. For centuries, Native Americans have made "dream catchers," a type of hanging mobile with a woven web and feathers. They trap bad dreams and allow good ones to pass through to the sleeper. People have always been fascinated by the mystery of dreams. **Let's Talk:** Do you often remember your dreams? Do you ever have the same dream over and over? Have you ever had a scary dream? What's your happiest dream of all time?

Accomplishments:

_____

_____

_____

Expectations:

_____

_____

_____

Family Matters:

_____

_____

_____

_____

_____

_____

_____

_____

PARENT-TO-PARENT

DREAM ON!

It may feel almost Freudian to attach too much significance to children's dreams; but as author Pam Spurr, Ph.D., says in her book, *Understanding Your Child's Dreams* (New York: Sterling Publishing Company, 1999), "By exploring your child's dreams you are valuing something that is uniquely theirs, giving them the message that you are interested in their hopes and ambitions, their inner life."

Week of: __ / __ / __ Through: __ / __ / __   Menus

Monday

A.M.   P.M.

Tuesday

A.M.   P.M.

Wednesday

A.M.   P.M.

Thursday

A.M.   P.M.

Friday

A.M.   P.M.

Saturday

A.M.   P.M.

Sunday

A.M.   P.M.

TV TURNOFFS

Parents can feel that keeping up with which shows are "okay" for kids to watch versus which are "not okay" is a big job. What is considered harmless in some families is on the restricted list at another home. While the content of programming has always been an issue for parents, the TV-Turnoff Network (*www.tvturnoff.org*) is concerned with the sheer amount of television watched. This grassroots effort encourages viewers to take a week off from television each April, in part to increase interaction within families. **Let's Talk:** Could we do without television for a week? A month? How about a whole summer? What are some other activities we could do instead? **Tip:** See "Free—or Nearly Free—Summer Activities" on page 115 for additional ideas. Many are doable year-round.

Accomplishments:

_____

_____

_____

Expectations:

_____

_____

_____

Family Matters:

_____

_____

_____

_____

_____

_____

_____

_____

_____

PARENT-TO-PARENT

CENSORED

There was a time when cartoons were intended strictly for young audiences, so they at least were free from controversy. But with the advent of animated shows for adults such as *South Park*, parents have had to develop a keener sense for what is acceptable and age-appropriate for their children. Make sure you are attentive to the content of the cartoons your child watches.

Week of: __ / __ / __ Through: __ / __ / __   Menus

Monday

A.M.   P.M.

Tuesday

A.M.   P.M.

Wednesday

A.M.   P.M.

Thursday

A.M.   P.M.

Friday

A.M.   P.M.

Saturday

A.M.   P.M.

Sunday

A.M.   P.M.

KEEP OUT!

Adults *and* kids need their own space, where they can play with their toys, read a book, write in their journals, or talk to their friends without interference. Knocking before entering, not eavesdropping on the telephone, and not using someone else's things without permission are ways of respecting other's boundaries. **Let's Talk:** How else can we respect each other's boundaries? How well do we respect each other's space? Is it ever permissible for parents to invade their child's privacy? Why or why not?

Accomplishments:

_____

_____

_____

Expectations:

_____

_____

_____

Family Matters:

_____

_____

_____

_____

_____

_____

_____

_____

_____

PARENT-TO-PARENT

DEAR DIARY

Keeping a journal is a good way for people of all ages to record memories, hopes, and dreams; relieve stress; and work out solutions to problems. Presenting a child with a diary, especially one with a lock, makes him or her feel grown-up and trustworthy. (Your child doesn't have to know you also want to encourage creative writing.)

Week of: __ / __ / __ Through: __ / __ / __   Menus

Monday
A.M.   P.M.

Tuesday
A.M.   P.M.

Wednesday
A.M.   P.M.

Thursday
A.M.   P.M.

Friday
A.M.   P.M.

Saturday
A.M.   P.M.

Sunday
A.M.   P.M.

GENDER BENDER

In many cultures, duties have traditionally been divided according to gender, with females typically assigned to homemaking and males assigned to responsibilities outside the home. Gender-based roles persist in some families, but with more women working outside the home and more untraditional families than ever, all children should learn to cook, clean, and take care of domestic responsibilities. And all children should learn to handle traditionally "male" duties such as bill paying, lawn care, and car maintenance. **Let's Talk:** Do the children in our family get equal opportunities to learn to cook, organize the paperwork, and help with repairs? If not, what can we do to change that?

Accomplishments:

_____
_____
_____

Expectations:

_____
_____
_____

Family Matters:

_____
_____
_____
_____
_____
_____
_____
_____
_____

NOT YOUR MAMMA'S HOME EC

Many middle schools and high schools offer courses in "Family and Consumer Science." These classes teach what Atlanta educator Debby Tarbutton calls contemporary "survival skills." Tarbutton believes that her classes instill a "my family needs me" feeling in her students.

Week of: __ / __ / __   Through: __ / __ / __

Menus

Monday
A.M.

P.M.

Tuesday
A.M.

P.M.

Wednesday
A.M.

P.M.

Thursday
A.M.

P.M.

Friday
A.M.

P.M.

Saturday
A.M.

P.M.

Sunday
A.M.

P.M.

THE GOLDEN RULE

Every major world religion adheres to some form of the "Golden Rule." In Christianity, it is "Do unto others as you would have them do unto you." In Buddhism, it is "Hurt not others in ways that you yourself would find harmful." In Hinduism, it is "Do not to another what is disagreeable to yourself." And in Judaism, it is "What is hateful to you, do not do to your fellowman. That is the entire Law, all the rest is commentary." **Let's Talk:** Is this how we treat each other in our family? Let's think about the last time two of us had an argument. Would we have behaved differently if we'd followed the Golden Rule?

Accomplishments:

_____

_____

_____

Expectations:

_____

_____

_____

Family Matters:

_____

_____

_____

_____

_____

_____

_____

_____

PARENT-TO-PARENT

DON'T TREAD ON ME

Young children are naturally egocentric. It's hard for them to imagine how another person feels. A concrete way to help them understand the Golden Rule is by frequently reminding them to put themselves "in the other person's shoes." As children grow up, they can make this practice a habit.

Week of: __ / __ / __ Through: __ / __ / __

Menus

Monday
A.M.   P.M.

Tuesday
A.M.   P.M.

Wednesday
A.M.   P.M.

Thursday
A.M.   P.M.

Friday
A.M.   P.M.

Saturday
A.M.   P.M.

Sunday
A.M.   P.M.

COUNT TO 10!

Small children are unable to control their emotions. When they are tired or hungry, they cry. Part of growing up is learning how to manage your reactions. For example, a preschooler might throw a tantrum if a brother or sister eats the last of his favorite cereal. But a 12-year-old is probably mature enough simply to choose another box. Sometimes even adults lose control. Have you ever seen a driver yell or shake a fist at another driver who did something annoying? **Let's Talk:** What are some strategies we can use to keep from blowing our tops? One of the most popular recommendations is counting to 10 before reacting. Do you think this works? If not, what else can you try?

Accomplishments:

_____

_____

_____

_____

Expectations:

_____

_____

_____

_____

Family Matters:

_____

_____

_____

_____

_____

_____

_____

_____

PARENT·TO·PARENT

DETACHMENT

We don't ordinarily think of "detachment" as a virtue. But in *The Family Virtues Guide: Simple Ways to Bring Out the Best in Our Children and Ourselves* (New York: Plume, 1997), authors Linda Kavelin Popov, Dan Popov, Ph.D., and John Kavelin describe its value this way: "Detachment means to feel what you feel but not have to act on the feeling unless you want to. It's kind of like standing beside yourself and watching what you are feeling as well as feeling it."

Week of: __ / __ / __ Through: __ / __ / __   Menus

Monday
A.M.

P.M.

Tuesday
A.M.

P.M.

Wednesday
A.M.

P.M.

Thursday
A.M.

P.M.

Friday
A.M.

P.M.

Saturday
A.M.

P.M.

Sunday
A.M.

P.M.

SHOW THEM THE MONEY

A hundred dollars means different things to children and adults. For kids, it could mean the world's greatest trip to the candy store. For parents, it can mean paying the utility bill. At any age, there are three ways to use money: spending, saving, and giving. **Let's Talk:** Could we use our money more wisely? How much of our money do we currently spend? Save? Give away? Should we set goals for saving and spending, or consider taking on a family charity? **Tip:** Use the "Family Bank & Trust" form on page 124 to help children keep track of their finances.

Accomplishments:

_____
_____
_____
_____

Expectations:

_____
_____
_____

Family Matters:

_____
_____
_____
_____
_____
_____
_____
_____
_____
_____

'TIS BETTER TO GIVE

DEAR SPONSOR FAMILY,

THANK YOU FOR YOUR LETTER. IT WAS SO NICE TO HEAR FROM YOU. HERE ARE PICTURES OF MY HOME.

FROM MARCO

Children are particularly interested in a charitable cause when they can relate to the recipients. Many nonprofit organizations match donors with an individual child so they can exchange letters and drawings. Check with a charity "watchdog" service, such as The American Institute of Philanthropy, 3450 North Lake Shore Drive, Suite 2802E, Chicago, IL 60657, (773) 529-2300, _www.charitywatch.org_, which helps donors make informed giving decisions.

Week of: __ / __ / __ Through: __ / __ / __   Menus

Monday

A.M.   P.M.

Tuesday

A.M.   P.M.

Wednesday

A.M.   P.M.

Thursday

A.M.   P.M.

Friday

A.M.   P.M.

Saturday

A.M.   P.M.

Sunday

A.M.   P.M.

BEST FRIENDS!

Do you have special friends you hope to know forever? Sometimes kids keep "best friends" for life—even after they grow up and have their own families. But what if your best friend decides to be "best friends" with somebody else? Or your best friend moves away? Your feelings may be hurt. You might feel embarrassed or sad. Sometimes the best way to heal the hurt of losing a friend is by being a friend to someone else. **Let's Talk:** What does it mean to be a true friend? What's one thing you can do to make friends with someone new?

Accomplishments:

_____

_____

_____

Expectations:

_____

_____

_____

Family Matters:

_____

_____

_____

_____

_____

_____

_____

Week of: __ / __ / __   Through: __ / __ / __   Menus

Monday

A.M.   P.M.

Tuesday

A.M.   P.M.

Wednesday

A.M.   P.M.

Thursday

A.M.   P.M.

Friday

A.M.   P.M.

Saturday

A.M.   P.M.

Sunday

A.M.   P.M.

LET'S MAKE A DEAL

In his online book, *Lessons on Lifemanship (bbll.com),* Bryan Bell describes the art of negotiation. Too often, he contends, people think of a good negotiator as someone who manages to get his or her way. He suggests a better way to negotiate: "Find out what the needs of the other person are and try to meet them without losing sight of your own goals." **Let's Talk:** When our family plans something together, are we able to negotiate? Let's talk about an upcoming event. If each person in the family got their way about some part of the plan, how might our agenda change? Things to consider include: timing, food or restaurant choice, indoor versus outdoor, and type of activity. Living with other people always includes compromise. Make it an art form!

Accomplishments: _____
_____
_____
_____

Expectations: _____
_____
_____

Family Matters: _____
_____
_____
_____
_____
_____
_____
_____

GIVE AND TAKE

Some parents are uncomfortable negotiating with their children. They fear they may be "smooth-talked" into changing their minds. But learning to negotiate is a skill that can help kids identify— and stick to—their principles.

SAND! GOLF! QUIET... PUTT-PUTT RIDES!

Week of: __ / __ / __ Through: __ / __ / __

Menus

Monday

A.M.   P.M.

Tuesday

A.M.   P.M.

Wednesday

A.M.   P.M.

Thursday

A.M.   P.M.

Friday

A.M.   P.M.

Saturday

A.M.   P.M.

Sunday

A.M.   P.M.

JUSTICE FOR ALL

In the book, *On Becoming Preteen Wise* (Simi Valley: Parent-Wise, 2000), authors Gary Ezzo, M.A., and Robert Bucknam, M.D., suggest giving children guidelines for an "appeals process," which helps resolve misunderstandings and prevent conflict. Some of the guidelines for using this process include:

- The appeal must be made to the parent giving the instructions.
- Parents should entertain an appeal only when the child comes with a respectful attitude.
- Appeals can be made only once.
- Children should use an agreed-upon phrase, such as: "May I appeal?"
- Parents must be fair and flexible.

Let's Talk: Would a process like this work for our family? What ground rules should we adopt for making appeals? For example, should kids be allowed to make appeals when a parent is driving?

Accomplishments:

_____

_____

_____

Expectations:

_____

_____

_____

Family Matters:

_____

_____

_____

_____

_____

APPEALING

Regardless of age, children can learn how to make their requests heard. Make it clear how and when kids are allowed to "make an appeal." Stay firm when they use an "unauthorized" method, such as whining or throwing a temper tantrum.

Week of: __ / __ / __ Through: __ / __ / __   Menus

Monday
A.M.   P.M.

Tuesday
A.M.   P.M.

Wednesday
A.M.   P.M.

Thursday
A.M.   P.M.

Friday
A.M.   P.M.

Saturday
A.M.   P.M.

Sunday
A.M.   P.M.

THANKS TO YOU

Often, we think of writing thank-you notes as a chore. After all, didn't we thank the giver in person when we received the present? And when you see someone all the time, writing him or her a note may seem awfully formal. But thank-you notes are about more than fulfilling an obligation. In *The Thank You Book for Kids: Hundreds of Creative, Cool, and Clever Ways to Say Thank You!* (Atlanta, GA: Longstreet Press, 2001), 15-year-old Ali Spizman lists 16 different uses for thank-you notes, including cheering someone up, complimenting them, encouraging someone to keep up the good work, and letting people know they are missed—in addition to just acknowledging a gift. **Let's Talk:** When is the last time you received something you were grateful for, either a gift, a kind word, or a thoughtful deed? Did you send a thank-you note? **Tip:** Use the "Thank-You List" on page 122 to help you keep track of gifts received and thank-you notes sent.

Accomplishments:

Expectations:

Family Matters:

PARENT-TO-PARENT

'TIS BLESSED TO RECEIVE

Whenever you give or receive special thanks, be sure to share the moment with your children. When they see how much kind words mean to you, they will understand and learn the power of gratitude.

thanks!

Week of: __ / __ / __ Through: __ / __ / __   Menus

Monday

A.M.   P.M.

Tuesday

A.M.   P.M.

Wednesday

A.M.   P.M.

Thursday

A.M.   P.M.

Friday

A.M.   P.M.

Saturday

A.M.   P.M.

Sunday

A.M.   P.M.

BEDTIME BATTLES

Somebody's always sleepy when families are a mix of Night Owls and Morning Larks. Even though individuals may need different amounts of sleep, everyone functions best when they've gotten enough shut-eye. Young children need 10 to 12 hours. Middle schoolers and adolescents need just over nine hours. Most adults need eight. The brain needs sleep like the body needs food. Without it, a person doesn't think clearly, easily gets in bad moods, and becomes forgetful. **Let's Talk:** Are we getting enough sleep? Do our family Morning Larks interfere with the Night Owls, or vice versa? Does everyone have an appropriate bedtime? If not, what are some ways we can help each other get to bed at a reasonable hour?

Accomplishments:

_____

_____

_____

Expectations:

_____

_____

_____

Family Matters:

_____

_____

_____

_____

_____

_____

_____

_____

PARENT·TO·PARENT

GOOD NIGHTS

Though children's evening schedules often get more complicated as they grow older, observing regular bedtime rituals helps kids relax and fall asleep more easily. Few people can doze off the minute their heads hit the pillow. Take time for a warm bath, a bedtime story, or an evening prayer.

Week of: __ / __ / __ Through: __ / __ / __   Menus

Monday

A.M.   P.M.

Tuesday

A.M.   P.M.

Wednesday

A.M.   P.M.

Thursday

A.M.   P.M.

Friday

A.M.   P.M.

Saturday

A.M.   P.M.

Sunday

A.M.   P.M.

MUST-HAVES

We are bombarded with advertisements insisting we must have the latest this or the hottest that. In fact, we need to have one—whether it's the latest video game, toy, sports car, or pair of shoes—right away! But how many of these things will we still want a month from now? A year? Advertisements make us believe that having certain things will make us happy. **Let's Talk:** What are some ways advertisers try to appeal to parents? Kids? Teenagers? What are the marketing executives' goals? Do they really want us to be happy, or do they just want us to buy their products?

Accomplishments:

_____
_____
_____
_____

Expectations:

_____
_____
_____
_____

Family Matters:

_____
_____
_____
_____
_____
_____
_____
_____
_____

PARENT-TO-PARENT

WISE BUYS

TEEN HYPE!

WHAT'S HOT!

Help your children learn to be critical consumers and understand how advertising can influence purchases. Whenever you're watching TV or reading a magazine, point out how the music, graphics, and models are chosen to reinforce a product's image. Kids won't stop wanting things, but they will develop into wiser consumers.

Week of: __ / __ / __ Through: __ / __ / __   Menus

Monday

A.M.   P.M.

Tuesday

A.M.   P.M.

Wednesday

A.M.   P.M.

Thursday

A.M.   P.M.

Friday

A.M.   P.M.

Saturday

A.M.   P.M.

Sunday

A.M.   P.M.

TIES THAT BIND

Rituals and traditions help bind families together and provide a sense of identity. These can be as simple as baking cookies or as complex as a Passover seder. In her book *The Shelter of Each Other: Rebuilding Our Families* (New York: Penguin Putnam, 1996), Mary Pipher writes, "Making school lunches, tying shoes, walking the dog, doing the dishes—any act that's done with love becomes a ritual." She then continues, "Saying grace is a ritual, as are Sunday dinners, toasts, and good-bye kisses. Reading aloud as a family is a lovely custom, once very common and now quite unusual. Anything can be a ritual if the family puts energy into making it meaningful. Ritual sanctifies time." **Let's Talk:** What are some of our families' most treasured rituals? Are there any new rituals we'd like to start?

Accomplishments:

_____

_____

_____

Expectations:

_____

_____

_____

Family Matters:

_____

_____

_____

_____

_____

_____

_____

PARENT-TO-PARENT

SWEET REPEATS

Parents are often surprised at how quickly children latch on to family rituals. Even if you've done something only two or three times, you're likely to hear your children tell their peers, "We do this every year...."

Week of: __ / __ / __   Through: __ / __ / __   Menus

Monday

A.M.   P.M.

Tuesday

A.M.   P.M.

Wednesday

A.M.   P.M.

Thursday

A.M.   P.M.

Friday

A.M.   P.M.

Saturday

A.M.   P.M.

Sunday

A.M.   P.M.

Tools

Summer Fun

What are we going to do this summer? Let's brainstorm the possibilities.

Places to Go

Where do we want to go that's close to home? (The zoo? A ball game? The park?) What are some special events coming up? (Fourth of July celebration? Outdoor concerts? Festivals? The county fair?) Do we want to go out of town? *Tip:* See the "Trip or Vacation Planner" on pages 116–117.

_____ _____

_____ _____

_____ _____

_____ _____

People to See

Family? Family friends? Kids' friends to invite over? Neighbors?

_____ _____

_____ _____

_____ _____

_____ _____

Things to Do

What are some projects we've been wanting (or needing) to do? (Build a bird house? Sew curtains? Bake a cake? Learn to play chess? Clean out the garage? Plant flowers or a vegetable garden?) Do we have any summer traditions? (Snow cones at the fairgrounds? Block parties with the neighbors? Catching fireflies?)

_____ _____

_____ _____

_____ _____

Free—Or Nearly Free—Summer Activities

Some of the best fun is "invented"! When boredom strikes, don't pull out the television guide, pull out this list! Add some of your family's own favorite ideas. (What did Mom or Dad do in the summer when they were kids?)

1. **Have a backyard picnic.** If you don't have a backyard, take a picnic to a nearby spot where you can enjoy the scenery.

2. **Play games with a garden hose.** Make a "bridge" to walk under. Do the "limbo." See how high you can jump over the stream of water. Hook up a sprinkler and run through it.

3. **Use chalk.** Draw hopscotch or art on the sidewalk or driveway.

4. **Lie on your back and look for objects in the clouds.** What shapes do you see?

5. **Count stars.** Check out a library book on the constellations and see if you can identify major ones in your night sky.

6. **Pick flowers and press them in an old phone book.** On a rainy day (after about three weeks), use them to make bookmarks. (Brush on a coating of watered-down craft glue as a "varnish.")

7. **Make frozen treats using craft sticks and fruit juice in paper cups.** Try making a mixture with yogurt and juice, too.

8. **Make a simple map of your neighborhood.** Talk about what a "bird's eye view" means.

9. **Create a family collage.** Dig up all those extra prints from double sets of photographs.

10. **Make paper airplanes and see how far they fly.** Test variations on the one that flies farthest. What design features make the plane go farther? Straighter?

11. **Make a miniature world using natural objects.** Find an old box or the hollow of a tree to create your tiny universe.

12. **Stage a simple play or puppet show.** Check out a book from the library on how to make your own puppets.

13. **Create an obstacle course.** See who can go through fastest.

14. **Check out a book on how to create a terrarium.** Start building one!

15. **Write a letter.** Send one to a friend or relative whom you rarely see.

16. **Make a flip book.** (If you use self-stick notes and draw small stick figures, they can still be used for their original purpose!)

17. **Choose a charity and then figure out a way to raise money for the organization.** (Make it simple: sell lemonade, walk neighbors' dogs, etc.) Or just raise awareness—make a flyer to hand out and inform people about how they can help your cause.

18. **Make your own fitness course with exercise stations.** You can do this inside or outside; place instructions for each station on the floor, table, chair, or wherever is handy.

19. **Start a book club.** You can find instructions online or at your library.

20. **Make your own tie-dye T-shirt.** (Messy, but cool.)

Trip or Vacation Planner

Brainstorming . . .

Here are some fun questions for the family to discuss:

- If you had a magical machine that could take you anywhere in the world, where would you go? Why?

- Which of your closest friends or relatives DO NOT live nearby? What are your favorite memories of visiting with them?

- What are some places in your state that you've always wanted to see? In your region? In other parts of the country? When is the best time of year to visit those places?

- What types of trips do you like best: seeing new sights, relaxing at a park or at the beach, enjoying the outdoors, learning about history, or exploring a big city?

- Where do you like to stay: with family or friends, in a hotel, in a cabin, in a tent?

- What do you like to eat? Do you like to do the cooking yourself? Eat in a cafeteria? Eat in a fancy restaurant? Try foods from other countries?

- What do you like to do? Go to sporting events? Participate in sports? Go on hikes? Attend performances? Go to museums? Shop? Visit with friends? Absolutely nothing?

- What's the best trip you ever had? What made it special?

Now, for some serious planning . . .

Possible trips or vacations	Pros	Cons	Dates	Cost	Transportation
_____	_____	_____	_____	_____	_____
_____	_____	_____	_____	_____	_____
_____	_____	_____	_____	_____	_____
_____	_____	_____	_____	_____	_____
_____	_____	_____	_____	_____	_____
_____	_____	_____	_____	_____	_____
_____	_____	_____	_____	_____	_____
_____	_____	_____	_____	_____	_____
_____	_____	_____	_____	_____	_____
_____	_____	_____	_____	_____	_____
_____	_____	_____	_____	_____	_____

Camp Planner

Camps, whether day camps or sleep-away camps, are a great way to meet new friends, have fun, and learn skills like canoeing, crafts, swimming, drama, or tennis. Brainstorm opportunities in your community. Good places to check for relatively inexpensive programs include the YMCA, the YWCA, religious organizations, nature centers, museums, parks, neighborhood centers, and educational institutions. Local parenting tabloids often publish lists of activities as early as February. Here's a page to keep track of the possibilities.

Place	Dates	Days/Hours	Extended Care (yes/no)	Cost	Transportation (yes/no)

June	July	August

Our Family's Top Ten Summer Memories

1. _____

2. _____

3. _____

4. _____

5. _____

6. _____

7. _____

8. _____

9. _____

10. _____

Attach the kids' drawings or family photos of fun summer times in the space below, or start a journal or notebook to record more summer memories.

Celebrations

In the book *The Shelter of Each Other: Rebuilding Our Families* (New York: Ballantine, 1997), Mary Pipher, Ph.D., writes: "It's important that national holidays be celebrated in the family's own way. Too often now holidays and celebrations mean buying a card and some candy. There's nothing wrong with that, but the more energy that the family puts into designing a meaningful celebration, the more powerful it becomes."

On the other hand, celebrations don't have to be elaborate to be meaningful. For example, if you feel compelled to bake six different kinds of cookies and decorate every room, you will probably be too exhausted to enjoy the day. Here is a planner for organizing your family's celebrations. Photocopy this blank form to use for all different types of events. Have fun!

Occasion: _____

Date: _____

Family Traditions: _____

Favorite Stories to Read or Tell: _____

What We Want to Say: _____

What We Want to Do: _____

Where We Want to Go: _____

Other Considerations: _____

_____

_____

_____

Party Planner

Is your family throwing a party? Here is a page to help you plan your special event!

Event: _____

Date: _____

Brainstorm ideas for the following elements:

Theme: _____

Decorations: _____

Invitation Design: _____

Music: _____

Games: _____

Food: _____

Drinks: _____

Favors: _____

Rain Plan: _____

Other: _____

_____

_____

Thank-You List

Giver	Gift	Date Received	Date Note Sent

Chore Chart

Copy this page as needed to keep track of everyone's chores.

_____'s Job's	Week of: _____							
Chore	# times/week	S	M	T	W	T	F	S

_____'s Job's	Week of: _____							
Chore	# times/week	S	M	T	W	T	F	S

From *Our Family Meeting Book: Fun and Easy Ways to Manage Time, Build Communication, and Share Responsibility Week by Week* by Elaine Hightower and Betsy Riley, copyright © 2002. Free Spirit Publishing Inc., Minneapolis, MN; 866/703-7322; *www.freespirit.com*. This page may be photocopied for individual or small group work only.

Family Bank & Trust

Does your family lose track of how much money everyone has? Here's an easy way for parents to "pay" their kids for chores or allowances, even if they don't have cash on hand. This is also a helpful way for kids to "deposit" money they earn or receive as gifts. Photocopy this page for each child.

Account Holder: _____

Date	Amount Withdrawn/Purpose	Amount Deposited/Source	Balance
	/	/	
	/	/	
	/	/	
	/	/	
	/	/	
	/	/	
	/	/	
	/	/	
	/	/	
	/	/	
	/	/	
	/	/	

Resources

Books

Building Moral Intelligence: The Seven Essential Virtues that Teach Kids to Do the Right Thing by Michele Borba, Ed.D. (San Francisco: Jossey-Bass, Wiley, 2001). Nationally known educator provides a practical, hands-on approach for helping parents teach their children the seven essential virtues that make up moral intelligence: empathy, conscience, self-control, respect, kindness, tolerance, and fairness.

Family Rules: Helping Stepfamilies and Single Parents Build Happy Homes by Jeannette Lofas, C.S.W. (New York: Kensington Books, 1998). This book was created specifically for blended families to help establish rules that will establish lasting harmony. Great handbook for *any* family to use.

The Family Virtues Guide: Simple Ways to Bring Out the Best in Our Children and Ourselves by Linda Kavelin Popov, Dan Popov, and John Kavelin (New York: Plume, 1997). Developed as part of The Virtues Project, its mission is to develop multicultural programs for helping people live by their highest values, this resource provides chapters for helping children and adults develop 52 important virtues. Each chapter discusses the meaning of the virtue and why it's important, provides discussion tips, and suggests signs of success.

How to Talk So Kids Will Listen & Listen So Kids Will Talk by Adele Faber and Elaine Mazlish (New York: Avon Books, 1980). This book has lots of examples, cartoons, exercises, and easy-to-understand illustrations about enhancing communication between children and adults.

The Hurried Child by David Elkind (Cambridge, MA: Perseus, 1989). This updated edition of Elkind's landmark book explores how parents' desire for children to "achieve" has pressured them into growing up too soon. He suggests ways to encourage appropriate development while preserving the freedom of childhood.

The Intentional Family: Simple Rituals to Strengthen Family Ties by William J. Doherty (New York: Avon Books, 1997). Doherty's crystal-clear vision of "parenting with intention" is a step-by-step manual to creating a rich family life.

The Kid's Guide to Service Projects by Barbara A. Lewis (Minneapolis: Free Spirit Publishing, 1995). This book offers practical suggestions for young peoples' service projects, plus advice on specific tasks such as taking a survey, ways to fundraise, and how to lobby.

KidStress: What it Is, How it Feels, How to Help by Georgia Witkin, Ph.D. (New York: Viking Press, 1999). Dr. Witkin's study of 800 boys and girls reveals the causes of stress for children along with effective strategies for dealing with pressures facing modern kids.

On Becoming Preteen Wise by Gary Ezzo, M.A., and Robert Bucknam, M.D. (Simi Valley: Parent-Wise, 2000). For this critical developmental period (ages 10–14), the authors advise parents to transition from parenting by "authority" to parenting by "influence" in order to develop their child's decision-making potential.

The Over-Scheduled Child: Avoiding the Hyper-Parenting Trap by Alvin Rosenfeld, M.D., and Nicole Wise (New York: St. Martin's Griffin, 2001). A must-read in today's society, this book encourages parents to listen to their inner voices and resist the pressure to push too hard.

Parents Do *Make a Difference: How to Raise Kids with Solid Character, Strong Minds and Caring Hearts* by Michele Borba, Ed.D. (San Francisco: Jossey-Bass, Wiley, 1999). Educator and parent Michele Borba shares a practical, hands-on approach for helping children develop eight skills necessary for success: positive self-esteem, cultivating strengths, communicating, problem solving, getting along, goal setting, not giving up, and caring.

The Parent's Toolshop by Jody Johnston Pawel (Springboro, OH: Ambris Publishing, 2000). Counselor and educator shares a field-tested "Universal Blueprint" for helping develop problem-solving skills, communication, character, and self-esteem.

Positive Discipline A–Z by Jane Nelsen, Ed.D., Lynn Lott, M.A., M.F.C.C., and H. Stephen Glenn, Ph.D. (Rocklin, CA: Prima Publishing, 2000). The authors apply their popular "positive discipline" approach to 26 everyday parenting problems.

Raising an Emotionally Intelligent Child by John Gottman (New York: Fireside Books, 1997). Gottman's "emotion-coaching" process gives parents techniques for helping kids understand and deal with emotions in a healthy, constructive way.

Raising Self-Reliant Children in a Self-Indulgent World by H. Stephen Glenn and Jane Nelsen, Ed.D. (Rocklin, CA: Prima Publishing, 2000). Noted educators review cultural forces eroding family values and share principles of positive discipline. They also teach ways to improve self-esteem, communication skills, judgement, and character.

Saving Childhood: Protecting Our Children from the National Assault on Innocence by Michael Medved and Diane Medved, Ph.D. (New York: HarperCollins, 1999). Contending that childhood is under attack from all sides, the Medveds seek to restore for children the three components of innocence: security, a sense of wonder, and optimism.

The 7 Habits of Highly Effective Families by Stephen R. Covey (New York: St. Martin's Griffin, 1998). Best-selling author applies his seven principles to family life. He contends that strong families don't just happen but require effort and dedication by all members.

The Shelter of Each Other by Mary Pipher, Ph.D. (New York: Penguin Putnam, 1996). In this follow-up book to her popular *Reviving Ophelia,* Pipher discusses the cultural influences eroding today's family life. She also shares ways to strengthen and develop this most vital institution.

Simplify Your Life with Kids: 100 Ways to Make Family Life Easier and More Fun by Elaine St. James (Kansas City: Andrews McMeel Publishing, 1997). The author provides one hundred entries for parents wanting to get back to the basics. The book has well-organized chapters with several very short and to-the-point sections in each.

Take Back Your Kids: Confident Parenting in Turbulent Times by William J. Doherty (Notre Dame, IN: Sorin Books, 2000). In this follow-up book, Doherty encourages parents to resist "going with the flow" and to set the limits kids need.

The Thank You Book for Kids: Hundreds of Creative, Cool, and Clever Ways to Say Thank You! by Ali Lauren Spizman (Atlanta, GA: Longstreet Press, 2001). Written by a teenager for kids, this slender volume suggests fun, creative, and easy ways to say thank you. It also explains why gratitude is important and includes letters from famous people like Hillary Rodham Clinton and popular juvenile author R.L. Stine.

Too Much of a Good Thing: Raising Children of Character in an Indulgent Age by Dan Kindlon, Ph.D. (New York: Hyperion, 2001). Kindlon brings attention to the recent epidemic of children who are "undernourished," despite their abundant surroundings. Hard-hitting but accessible writing, Kindlon personally faces all of the challenges he describes.

Understanding Your Child's Dreams by Pam Spurr, Ph.D. (New York: Serling Publishing Co., Inc., 1999). This book is a fun look into children's inner lives. Using this book is a great way to foster intimacy and imagination.

What Works with Children edited by Marshall P. Duke and Sara B. Duke (Atlanta: Peachtree, 2000). A collection of essays from educators, counselors, clergy, librarians, and physicians who have spent their lives working with children, they share their wisdom and experience about the most effective ways to raise children.

Web Sites and Organizations

The Family Education Network
www.familyeducation.com
A comprehensive network of articles, resources, links, and shopping, this site seeks to help parents, teachers, and students of all ages take control of their learning and make it part of their everyday lives.

The National Parenting Center
22801 Ventura Boulevard, Suite 110
Woodland Hills, CA 91367
1-800-753-6667
www.tnpc.com
This organization provides parenting advice from child-rearing authorities. Browse reading rooms for answers to specific questions and the latest medical, behavioral, and educational information. Become a member and receive *ParenTalk,* a monthly magazine from experts in childcare fields.

Parent Center
www.parentcenter.com
This site offers not only a lot of great practical information about children's health and education, but also games, activities, and family vacation ideas. Other features include an activity planner, an immunization scheduler, and a behavior problem solver.

Parenting.com
www.parenting.com
With articles on health, nutrition, and the trials of raising children in today's popular culture, this online resource covers a wide range of topics. Expert advice, product reviews, and quick tips make this a good resource for parents without a lot of time.

Parenting.org
www.parenting.org
Parenting.org was developed by the Girls and Boys Town National Resource and Training Center, offering guidance and advice to parents with kids of all ages. Divided into four separate periods of growth, find pertinent articles and advice about the health, education, and safety of children.

Parenting Resources for the 21st Century
www.parentingresources.ncjrs.org
Parenting Resources covers the full spectrum of parenting. The site has links to material on a variety of topics, such as infant development, organized sports, domestic violence, nutrition, volunteer activities, learning disabilities, and mental health.

Search Institute
The Banks Building
615 First Avenue NE, Suite 125
Minneapolis, MN 55413
1-800-888-7828
www.searchinstitute.com
Search Institute is a nonprofit and nonsectarian organization that works toward improving the well-being of adolescents and children. Providing up-to-date research on what kids need, Search works with community leaders and state and national organizations toward instilling youth with values that will ensure they live fulfilling lives.

Index

About the Authors

Elaine Hightower: Elaine has always enjoyed coming up with fun, creative projects. Before she was married and had children, she enjoyed traveling. She lived in Los Angeles for two years in her twenties, then moved to Switzerland to attend Art Center College of Design. There she lived with a French family, even though she didn't speak French. Now she prefers mostly staying home with her family and pets (three dogs, two cats, two birds, one hamster, many fish).

For the past 10 years Elaine has been a part of the editorial team of the award-winning regional publication, *Atlanta* Magazine. Awards for *Atlanta* under her art directorship included the prestigious Ozzie award for Best Overall Design (for consumer magazines with circulation under 100,000), the Magazine Association of Georgia's Gold Award for Best Single Issue, the Gold Award for General Excellence, and the Silver Award for Best Design. Currently Elaine designs special publications for the company, along with writing and art directing select items for the monthly magazine. Recently Elaine has developed, with Betsy's help, several products in the official merchandise line of the Lewis & Clark Bicentennial.

Elaine lives in Atlanta with her husband, Ed, and their two children, Gus and Rachel.

Betsy Riley: During Betsy's 20-year career in journalism, she has written about everything from laser surgery to mountain arts and crafts. Through interviewing hundreds of interesting people, Betsy has grown to appreciate a wide variety of people, places and things. When her kids were younger, they would pile in the car and go to interviews with her. They met every blacksmith in North Georgia. Now that her sons, Daniel and Mikey, are older, they've got schedules of their own. So Betsy's spending more time at the ballpark than writing travel stories.

Betsy has been a freelance writer and editor since her oldest son, Daniel, was born. She has written for regional magazines like *Southern Living* as well as national publications like *Ladies' Home Journal* and *Parenting*. Like Elaine, Betsy's longest association has been with *Atlanta* Magazine, where she is currently editor of special publications. Writing this book has allowed Betsy to use her long-dormant academic background in counseling and education. She has a master's degree in religious education, earned at three different seminaries: Gordon-Conwell in South Hamilton, MA, Columbia in Decatur, GA, and Candler School of Theology in Atlanta.

Betsy lives in Marietta, Georgia, with her sons and her husband, Mark.

Check out the *Our Family Meeting* Web site at *www.OurFamilyMeeting.com*.

Other Great Books from Free Spirit!

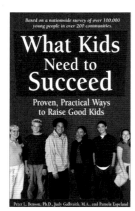

What Kids Need to Succeed

Proven, Practical Ways to Raise Good Kids

Revised, Expanded, and Updated Edition

by Peter L. Benson, Ph.D., Judy Galbraith, M.A., and Pamela Espeland

Our new edition of a proven best-seller identifies 40 developmental "assets" kids need to lead healthy, productive, positive lives, then gives them more than 900 suggestions for building their own assets at home, at school, in the community, and in the congregation. *Parents' Choice* approved. For parents, teachers, community and youth leaders, and teens.

$6.95; 256 pp.; softcover; 4⅛" x 6⅞"

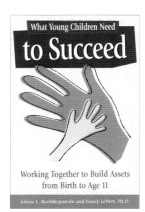

What Young Children Need to Succeed

Working Together to Build Assets from Birth to Age 11

by Jolene L. Roehlkepartain and Nancy Leffert, Ph.D.

Based on ground-breaking research, this book helps adults create a firm foundation for children from day one. You'll find hundreds of practical, concrete ways to build 40 assets in four different age groups. Comprehensive, friendly, and easy-to-use, this book will make anyone an asset builder and a positive influence in children's lives. For parents, teachers, all other caring adults, and children.

$11.95; 320 pp.; softcover; illus.; 5¼" x 8"

Raising Healthy Children Day by Day

366 Readings for Parents, Teachers, and Caregivers, Birth to Age 5

by Jolene L. Roehlkepartain

Daily readings support adults who live and work with infants, toddlers, and preschoolers and who want to build young children's developmental assets—positive things all kids need in their lives. Based on groundbreaking research, each reading helps adults promote social skills, positive values, boundaries and expectations, family support, and more—one day at a time. Simple, practical, and inspiring.

$10.95; 416 pp.; softcover; 4¼" x 6¼"

Visit us on the Web!
www.freespirit.com

Stop by anytime to find our Parents' Choice Approved catalog with fast, easy, secure 24-hour online ordering; "Ask Our Authors," where visitors ask questions—and authors give answers—on topics important to children, teens, parents, teachers, and others who care about kids; links to other Web sites we know and recommend; fun stuff for everyone, including quick tips and strategies from our books; and much more! Plus our site is completely searchable so you can find what you need in a hurry. Stop in and let us know what you think!

To place an order or to request a free catalog of SELF-HELP FOR KIDS®
and SELF-HELP FOR TEENS® materials, please write, call, email, or visit our Web site:

Free Spirit Publishing Inc.
217 Fifth Avenue North • Suite 200 • Minneapolis, MN 55401
toll-free 800.735.7323 • local 612.338.2068 • fax 612.337.5050
help4kids@freespirit.com • www.freespirit.com